Welcome back – After the holidays

1 Where were they? ▸ p. 7

a) *Where were the Bristol kids in the holidays? Who says what? Match the pictures and the speech bubbles.*

We had great holidays. I was in the pool or on the beach every day. Majorca is really great!

Bristol is a great place in summer. We stayed at home because we had lots of nice guests at the B&B.

We were in a caravan by the sea. It was fun and we met a nice girl, a very nice girl.

Hello! Hello! I was at home with Jack, but we had some nice trips in the country. Nice trips. Nice trips.

I had fantastic holidays. I went to New York! My cousi v lives there.

b) *Now write sentences about the kids and Polly with* was *or* were*.*

Jack was at home in Bristol. ____________ *An* ____________

____________ ____________ ____________

0101 ____________ ____________ ____________

2 WORDS Holiday words ▸ p. 7

Write the missing words. ▸ What's the word in the yellow boxes?

1 Let's play football on the *beach* ____!

2 Let's write a funny ____________ to Grandma!

3 We were in a nice ____________ by the sea.

4 We stayed at a small house in the ____________.

5 The ____________ from our window was fantastic.

6 The ____________ was too cold, so we went swimming in the pool.

7 New York looked fantastic from the ____________.

8 Majorca is an ____________.

0102 ▸ It's a very nice place for holidays: ____________.

1	b	_	_	c	_					
2			_	_	s	_	_	_	_	_
3		_	_	_	_	v	_	_		
4	_	_	_	n	_	_	_	_	s	
5	v	_	_	_						
6		_	e	_						
7			p	_	_	n	_			
8		_	_	l	_	_	_			

3 WORDS What's the weather like? ▸ p. 8

Choose two correct words and write sentences.

cold • hot • sunny • rainy

It's hot and sunny.

windy • cloudy • rainy • cold

rainy • sunny • stormy • hot

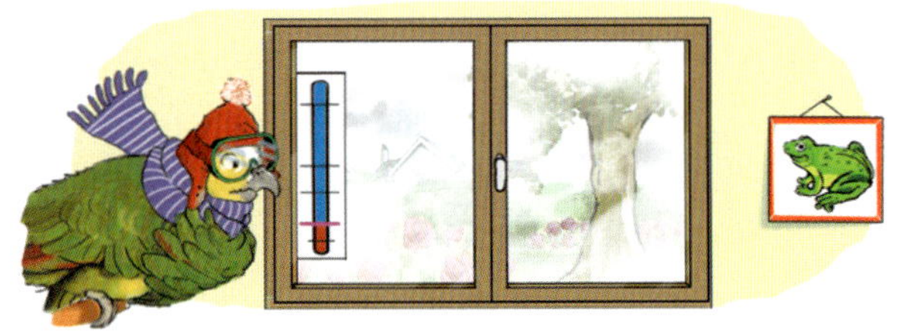

warm • sunny • cold • foggy

0203

Now you

Write three sentences about the weather.

Today the weather ______________________________.

I like it when ______________________________.

Yesterday it ______________________________.

4 Extra Countries ▸ p. 8 • p. 209

a) *Write the correct name and match. One country is not in the picture.*

P	A	N	I	S					Spain
T	I	L	A	Y					
N	F	A	E	C	R				
Y	R	N	E	G	A	M			
C	L	T	S	N	O	D	A		
T	A	R	A	L	S	U	I	A	
S	E	W	L	A					

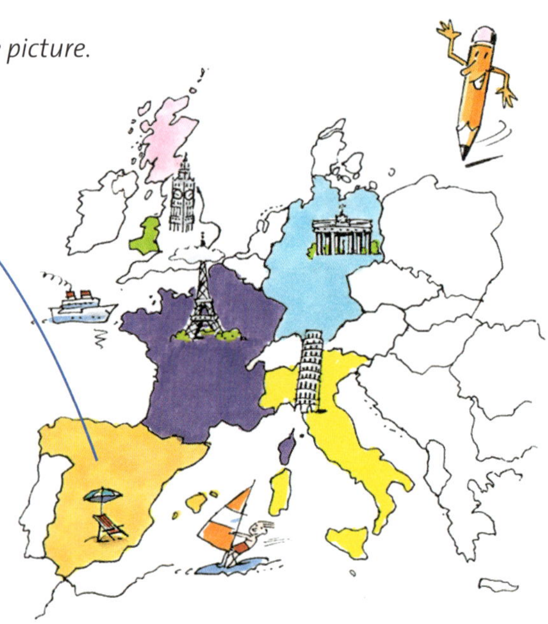

0204 ***b)*** *Which country isn't in the picture?* ______________

5 WORDS Holiday talk ▸ p. 9

Becky, Lucy, Florian and some friends are talking about their holidays.
Look at their photos. Where were they? Complete the sentences.

1

2

3

4

5

in a holiday flat by the sea • in the country • in the mountains • by car • by a lake • on the beach

1 *Becky* We were in Italy. It was great! We stayed *in a holiday flat by the sea.*

2 *Lucy* We were in Scotland. We went ____________ . We were in a caravan ____________ .
It was warm and sunny. We had lots of fun.

3 *Florian* I was in Germany at my uncle's house. He lives ____________ near Munich[1].

4 *Nick* We went to Germany too. We stayed in a holiday flat ____________ .

5 *Emma* We were in Spain. It was hot, so we were ____________ every day.

Rhyme time

Holidays are lots of fun,
You can swim in the sea,
You can play in the sun.
New places to see,
New things to do,
I like holidays,
What about you?

Now you

0305
0306

*Look at the photos in exercise **5** again. Where do you like to stay? In the mountains, by the sea or in the country? In a holiday flat or in a caravan? What's best and why? Write at least four sentences in your exercise book.*

[1]Munich [mju:nik] *München*

Unit 1 Back to school

1 WORDS Where are the school words? ▸ pp. 10–11

Find the mistakes. Cross out the wrong words in the lists and write them in the correct lists.

At school

~~dishwasher~~
notice board
washing machine
timetable
PE
station
bedroom
essays
Art Club
museum

At home

pets
bridge
classmates
teacher
parents
kitchen
bathroom
sports centre
doorbell
church

dishwasher

In my town or village

wardrobe
shops
library
fish bowl
morning break
houses
exercises
tower
Geography

0401

2 STUDY SKILLS Describing pictures ▸ pp. 10–11 • SF (p. 123)

Look at the postcard and complete the text on the next page.

0402
0403

Choose from:

at the top	on the right	on the left	in the middle	in the foreground
at the bottom	in the background			

At the top ________ of the postcard it says '*Welcome ...*'

________ there's a boy with a comic. ________ there's a girl with an ice cream.

________ you can see the sea – and a boat. ________ there's a little brown dog. ________ of the picture there are two children with a ball.

________ of the postcard it says '*... to sunny Cornwall!*'

3 LISTENING The Muddles

▸ *pp. 10–11* 🎧 2

a) *The Muddles have got six children:* **Max**, **Micky**, **Molly**, **Millie**, **Minnie** *and* **Maggie**. *But who's who? Listen and write the names in the boxes.*

b) *Now describe the photo. Use:* **between**, **in front of, ...**

Max is ________

____

____

____

____

4 WORDS Find the socks ▸ pp. 10–11

When the Carter-Browns were on holiday, Prunella put Emily's socks in lots of different places. Where are they? Choose the correct word and complete the sentences.

behind

between

in front of

near

next to

under

1 There's *a red sock near the door.*

2 There's ______________________________ wardrobe.

3 There's ______________________________ armchair.

4 There's ______________________________ computer.

5 There's ______________________________ books.

6 There's ______________________________ CDs.

Now you

Where are these things in your room: window, bed, wardrobe, desk/table, chair, clock, lamp? Use ***behind, between, in front of, near, next to*** *and* ***under****. Write at least five sentences in your exercise book.*

The window is between my bed and my desk.

5 PRONUNCIATION Vowel sounds ▸ p. 12 🎧 3

Listen and say the words. Colour the CDs with the same sound ***red*** *[ɜː],* ***green*** *[ɪə] or* ***blue*** *[eə].*

6 WORDS Find the new word

► p. 12

First write the missing word, then write the letter. The letters give you the answer to the question.

1 It was Ananda's first time on a ...	plane	(4)	N
2 American English for 'lift':		(3)	
3 Ananda and Dilip ... there together.		(4)	
4 American English for 'underground':		(6)	
5 The subway is fast, but not ...		(7)	
6 The ... was great – sun all the time.		(7)	
7 They ... the lift to the top of the Empire State Building.		(4)	

Question: Where did they go? – To ____________________.

7 PRONUNCIATION Which letters can't you hear?

► p. 12 4

Listen and say the words. Which letters can't you hear? Cross them out (X).

b~~u~~ilding | clothes | island | knee | talk | who | what | walk | climb | wrong | know | Science | write

0707

8 Extra REVISION A verb snake (Simple past: regular forms) ▸ p. 12 • GF 1a (p. 133)

Find the regular verbs and write them in the simple past form.

stayed

0808

9 WRITING Boring! (Linking words) ▸ p. 12 • SF (p. 129)

Tim's homework was: 'Write a story about a boring Saturday afternoon'. Write Tim's story.
*Use simple past forms from exercise **8**. You can change the order. Use time phrases too:* **first**, **then**, **after that**, **an hour later** ... *Ideas:* **football**, **watch kids**, **weather**, **rainy**, **help mum**, **clean bike**, **tidy room**, **wash car** ...

It was a boring Saturday afternoon, so I walked to the park with a friend. First we played

10 Find the verbs (Simple past: irregular forms) ► p. 13 • GF 1b (p. 133)

a) *Find the infinitives and the simple past forms. Write two lists.*

k	m	l	p	s	a	p	r	u	n
s	e	e	g	r	h	m	o	n	i
t	e	d	c	o	m	e	f	n	h
o	t	s	k	d	b	t	a	k	e
o	r	i	d	e	m	y	s	w	a
k	a	w	g	v	h	h	a	k	r
c	n	m	o	f	l	e	w	m	d
a	p	g	d	l	k	a	t	e	g
m	l	e	f	y	t	r	g	n	o
e	a	t	g	s	p	w	e	n	t

0910

Infinitive	Simple past
see	saw

b) *Now read what Florian says about a day in the holidays. Complete with simple past forms from a).*

One day in the holidays I __________ to a lake with my dad. We __________ our bikes and __________ some cheese sandwiches for lunch. We __________ a nice place for a picnic, so we __________ our sandwiches under a tree. In the afternoon we __________ two boys with a dog and a kite. The dog __________ and wanted to get[1] the kite, but it was windy so the kite __________ in the sky for at least ten minutes. Then suddenly it __________ down – on Dad's head.

[1] get [get] *kriegen*

11 Extra REVISION What don't they do? (Simple present: negative statements) ▸ p. 13

*The Muddles children don't always do what their parents say. Write sentences with **doesn't/don't**.*

clean her teeth • eat their breakfast • shout • *have a shower* • wash her face • make their beds

Max  *Max doesn't always have a shower.*

____

Millie  _______________

____

Maggie and Minnie  _______________

____

Millie  _______________

____

Molly and Micky  _______________

____

Mr and Mrs Muddles  _______________

1011 at their children – but today ...!

12 REVISION How were your holidays? (Simple past: be) ▸ p. 13 • GF 1 (p. 133)

*Complete the dialogue with **was**, **were**, **wasn't** or **weren't**.*

Prunella Where __________ you all?

Sophie We __________ on the island of Majorca.

Prunella __________ it boring without me?

Sophie No, it __________, Prunella. We __________ in a house with our own pool.

Prunella __________ your room nice, like our room at home?

Sophie Well, the rooms __________ big, but my room __________ very nice.

Prunella And __________ there any very nice poltergeists in it, like me?

Sophie No, there __________, Prunella. No poltergeists.

1012 *Prunella* Oh, so your holidays __________ very good ...

13 Poor Barnabas (Simple past: negative statements) ▸ p. 13 • GF 2 (p. 134)

Barnabas didn't have good holidays. Read why. Write the verbs in the simple past.

I didn't go __________ (go) to Italy with Tim and the Baxters. Tim __________ (take) me.

But I __________ (stay) at home with the neighbours. I stayed with Aunt Mildred.

She has got a big, old house – and a big, scary dog. The dog __________ (play) with me and

he __________ (give) me his food. I was a good pet, but Aunt Mildred __________ (talk)

to me much. I __________ (sit) on her sofa and I was so nice to her.

On the first day I took a nice dead mouse into the house for her. I put it on the kitchen table,

but she __________ (like) it. I don't know why, because it was a very big, dead mouse ...

1113

14 PRONUNCIATION Sounds ▸ p. 14 5

Listen to the words and match them to the correct sounds.

amazing	[dɪ'skrɪpʃn]	nothing	['æŋgri]
description	[ə'meɪzɪŋ]	subway	[mɪ'steɪk]
remember	['ɪtəli]	person	[dɪ'gri:]
caravan	['deɪndʒərəs]	angry	['nʌθɪŋ]
dangerous	[rɪ'membə]	degree	['pɜ:sn]
Italy	['kærəvæn]	mistake	['sʌbweɪ]

15 REVISION Do you like parties? (Simple present: yes/no questions) ▸ p. 14

There's an American boy in your Art Club. Ask questions about him and his sister.

1 like parties? Do you like parties? Does your sister like parties too?

2 do sport? ______

3 make models? ______

4 read comics? ______

16 The first day (Simple past: yes/no questions and short answers) ▸ p. 14 • GF 3 (p. 134)

Read A2 and A4 (pp. 13–14) in your student's book again. Then match.

1 Did Ananda and Sophie talk to Lesley?	No, they didn't.
2 Did Lesley talk to the girls?	No, he didn't.
3 Did Jack eat a chicken burger?	No, she didn't.
4 Did Dan get angry?	Yes, they did.
5 Did the girls go outside?	Yes, he did.
6 Did Lesley say 'Mind your own business'?	Yes, she did.

Rhyme time

A new school year
and lots to do,
New students, books,
new timetable too.
It's fun to laugh and
make new friends,
But I'm always happy
when the school day
ends ...

17 Questions for Ananda (Simple past: yes/no questions) ▸ p. 14 • GF 3 (p. 134)

Ananda's mum asked Ananda lots of questions about the first day of school. What did she ask?

1 you – see your friends? Did you see your friends?

2 they – talk about their holidays? ______

3 they – ask you about New York? ______

4 Mr Kingsley – give you the new timetable? ______

5 you – use new books? ______

1217 6 the teachers – give you homework? ______

Just for fun

18 More questions (Simple past: questions) ▸ p. 14 • GF 3 (p. 134)

*Emily's cousin asked her lots of questions about the holidays. Look at Emily's answers. Write her cousin's questions with **Where** (3x), **What** (3x), **Who**, **When**, **How**, **How long**.*

Questions:		Emily's answers:
1 ______		– We went to Majorca.
2 ______		– We went there by plane, of course.
3 ______		– We stayed for two weeks.
4 ______		– We stayed in a house near the sea.
5 ______	(do)	– We went swimming, we played volleyball on the beach, we went shopping …
6 ______		– I met some nice German people, and a very nice French boy too.
7 ______		– We saw lots of interesting places.
8 ______		– We came back two weeks ago.
9 ______	(buy)	– Just some small presents for my friends. Oh, and some nice earrings.
10 ______	(buy)	– In a great shop near the beach. Not expensive.

1318
1319

19 GETTING BY IN ENGLISH A new student ▸ p. 15

There's a new student from England in your class. She doesn't speak German. Ask her questions.

1 Frag sie, woher sie aus England kommt. ______

2 Frag sie, warum sie nach Deutschland kam. ______

3 Sag ihr, du wolltest nicht hierherkommen, ______

4 aber jetzt gefällt es dir hier wirklich gut. ______

5 Bitte sie, euch von London zu erzählen. ______

6 Frag sie, ob sie mit euch essen möchte. ______

20 WORKING WITH THE TEXT Saved! ▸ pp. 22–23

a) *Read the story on pp. 22–23 of your student's book again. Write the missing words. The letters in the boxes give you a place name from the story.* ▸ *What is it?*

1 Dan looked out to [s] __ __ .

2 Jody didn't know about the [ ] __ d __ __ .

3 Jody was a good __ __ [ ] __ __ __ __ .

4 Dan saw Jody __ a [ ] __ .

5 A __ __ f [ ] __ __ __ __ came to pull Jody out of the sea.

6 The lifeboatmen – and the twins – [ ] __ __ e __ Jody's life.

▸ The place name is __ __ __ __ __ __ .

b) *Put the pictures in the right order. Write 1–6 in the boxes.*

c) *Now you are Dan. Write a letter to Grandma Shaw about Jody. Use the simple past and write in your exercise book.*

first – have breakfast – caravan • after breakfast – go swimming • then – see – Jody – beach • we – play – football – other people, but – worry about – Jody – because – she – be – so far away • she – not know – tides • man with binoculars – see that Jody – be in trouble • Dad – call – lifeboat – mobile. • A few minutes later – lifeboat – come – St Ives. • men – pull – Jody – out of – sea • she – be – OK • we – go – St Ives – dad – see her

Dear Grandma

I must tell you what happened yesterday. Well, first we had breakfast in the caravan ...

1 What's the weather like?

1 It's ______________________.

2 ______________________

3 ______________________

4 ______________________

1501

2 That's wrong!

These sentences are wrong. Write them with **didn't**.

1 Lesley tried to be nice. ______________________

2 She wanted to come to Bristol. ______________________

3 Jack flew to New York. ______________________

1502 4 Jo ran to get help for Jody. ______________________

3 Ask Ananda questions.

Read Ananda's answers, then write your questions.

1 ______________________ – We went to New York.

2 ______________________ – We stayed for two weeks.

3 ______________________ – It was really hot on most days.

1503 4 ______________________ – Lots of things. We went up the Empire State Building, we went shopping, we went on a boat trip.

4 Describe the picture.

Where are they? Use: **between**, **behind**, **on the right**, **on the left**

1 Ali is ______________________.

2 Sue is ______________________.

3 Pat is ______________________.

1504 4 Ed is ______________________.

16 points

Now you

1505
1506
Write at least four sentences about the first day of school after the holidays. What did you do? What didn't you do?
Ideas: **get a new timetable**, **see your old friends**, **do a lot of work**, **talk about the holidays**, **get lots of homework**

Unit 2 What money can buy

1 STUDY SKILLS Learning words – Step 2 ▸ p. 27 • SF (p. 121)

a) *First, find four group words from the box and write them at the top of the lists. Then write the other words in the correct groups.*

months • July • knee • skirt • clothes • cloudy • shirt • shoulder • weather • countries • Scotland • leg • body • March • New Zealand • stormy • trousers • sunny • Turkey • toes • foggy • May • trainers • December • France

1 months	2	3	4	5
July				

1601

b) *Now find group words for these things.*

1	collecting things	reading	playing the guitar	making models	
2	pencil case	ruler	felt tip	rubber	
3	food	guests	invitations	presents	

2 LISTENING Becky's friends[1] ▸ p. 27 🎧 6

Becky is talking about her four best friends. Look, listen and tick (✓) the correct four boxes.

[1]sports gear ['spɔːts gɪə] *Sportsachen*

3 WORDS Our favourite clothes ▸ p. 27

a) *What are Tim and Becky wearing today? Write the clothes words.*

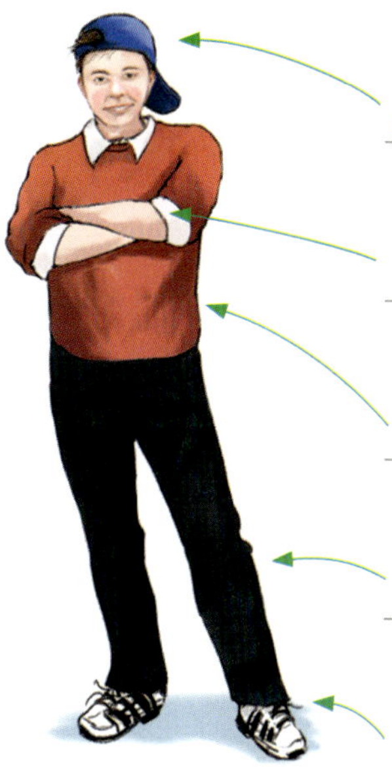

cap ______

______

______

______

______

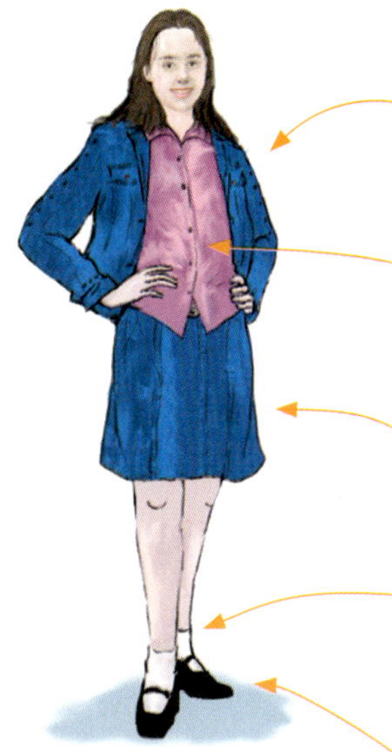

______

______

______

______

______

1703

b) *Now write about what they are wearing. Use colour words and* **long**, **short**, **a pair of**…

Tim is wearing a blue cap, a red ______

______

______

______

______

Now you

What are you wearing today? Write at least three sentences in your exercise book.

4 Is this your dictionary? (Possessive pronouns) ▸ p. 28

After school Mr Kingsley finds some things in 8PK's classroom. He asks Jack about them. Choose the correct word.

Mr K Is this your dictionary, Jack? It was on Lesley's desk.
Jack Well, maybe it's (his/hers), Mr Kingsley.
Mr K And here are some CDs. Are they (theirs/yours), Jack?
Jack No, they aren't (yours/mine). Oh, they're all rap. They must be the twins' CDs.
Mr K Well, yes, maybe they're (his/theirs). And what about these trainers under my desk?
Jack Oh, Jo lost his trainers yesterday. Maybe they're (ours/his).
Mr K OK. Fine. Yes, ermm … and then there's this exercise book. There's no name on it, but …
Jack Oh, that's (mine/ours), Mr Kingsley.
1704 *Mr K* Really? Well, … there's a funny picture of me in it – with pink hair and funny clothes. Jack? What's the matter? Is this exercise book (theirs/yours) – or isn't it?

5 It isn't mine (Possessive pronouns) ▸ p. 28

Tim wants to go to the park with Florian, but it's cold and windy.
Use **mine, yours, his, hers, ours, theirs, yours**.

Mrs Baxter Tim, it's windy. Take your cap. Here it is.

Tim But Mum, that isn't (my cap) ___mine___.

Florian, is it (your cap) ________?

Florian No, it isn't. (My cap) ________ is blue.

Tim Oh, so it isn't (our cap) ________.

Florian Well, Nick has got a cap like that. Maybe it's (his cap) ________.

Tim Becky has got a red cap too. Maybe it's (her cap) ________. And the neighbours' twins have got red caps. Maybe it's one of (their caps) ________.

Florian Try it on, Tim. Does it fit? Hey! It looks great! Now it's (your cap) ________!

Tim The wind! Oh, no! Where's the cap now?

Florian Look! It's up there, in that big tree! So now it's nobody's cap …

Just for fun

A: What are you doing?
B: I'm eating these chips.
A: But those chips were mine.
B: Yes, right. They were yours.

6 REVISION What did you do? (Simple past) ▸ p. 28 • GF 1–3 (pp. 133–134)

Fill in the correct form of the simple past.

Sophie When we were on holiday, I ___went___ (go) swimming every day.

Prunella Where ___did you go___ (you/go) swimming? In the sea?

Sophie No, we ________ (go) in the sea because it was often very windy. We ________ (like) our pool in the garden.

Prunella And what ________ (Emily/do) all day? (she/go) ________ shopping?

What ________ (she/buy)? Lots of presents for her friends?

Sophie Well, ________ (she/buy) presents. Just clothes, I think. Tops, a pair of trainers, some trousers, a skirt, some make-up …

Prunella Oh! Really! But you ________ (you/buy) presents for your friends, Sophie.

1806 And ________ (you/buy) a present for me?

Now you

What did you do in the holidays? Where did you go? Did you go shopping? What did you buy? Write at least three sentences in your exercise book.

7 Extra WORDS make or do? ▸ p. 28

a) *Match.*

your bed · tricks · breakfast · yoga · a poster · sport

make · do

a mess · a project · a cake · homework · an exercise

b) *Now fill in the right forms.*

doing • do (2x) • made • make • makes • making

Lucy What are you doing?

Becky I'm ______________ a poster for our Drama Club. Then I have to ______________ my Maths homework. Would you like some tea? I ______________ a chocolate cake yesterday too. Tim ate most of it.

Lucy Does Tim help in the kitchen? Can he ______________ cakes too?

Becky Not really. He just ______________ a mess. He always says he hasn't got much time because he's ______________ a project for school. But he finds time to ______________ sport every day.

1907

8 Extra REVISION We need some milk (some and any) ▸ p. 28

*What do Dan and Jo need to make these things? Write sentences with **some** or **any**.*

tea:

1 They need some tea and some milk. They don't need any

hamburgers:

2 ______________

fruit salad:

3 ______________

cheese sandwiches:

4 ______________

9 PRONUNCIATION Sounds at the end of words (Consonants) ▸ p. 28 7

Listen and write. Which sound do you hear at the end of the words?

[b] or [p]?	job [dʒɒ *b*]	club [klʌ ___]	stop [stɒ ___]
	drop [drɒ ___]	Rob [rɒ ___]	cap [kæ ___]
[g] or [k]?	bag [bæ *g*]	back [bæ ___]	leg [le ___]
	fog [fɒ ___]	look [lʊ ___]	big [bɪ ___]
[d] or [t]?	card [kɑː *d*]	looked [lʊk ___]	told [təʊl ___]
	dropped [drɒp ___]	heard [hɜː ___]	helped [help ___]

2009

10 How much ...? (much/many – more – most) ▸ p. 29

a) *Complete with* **much** *or* **many**.

Florian I don't get *much* pocket money, but I don't buy *many* things.

Tim Me too. I don't need ________ money because Mum buys my clothes and school things. I don't buy ________ comics now because my cousin gives me his. I buy chocolate, but not ________.

Florian Well, I don't buy ________ sweets, but I buy lots of ice cream in summer – and that's expensive!

Rhyme time

Fun with my pet,
A day with friends,
I'm always sad
when a good time ends.
I don't need much money,
Because, you see,
The things I like
Are always free.

● ***b)*** *Now make comparisons with* **more** *and* **the most**.

I buy a sports magazine every week, a comic and a computer magazine. I usually save two pounds of my pocket money.

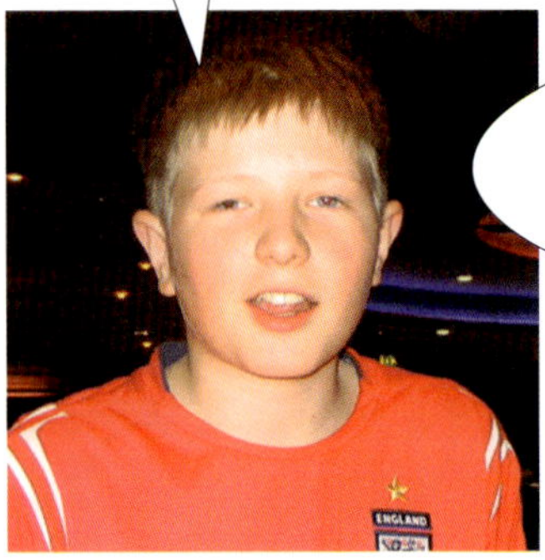

Florian

I buy a computer magazine and a pop magazine. I save three pounds every week.

Lucy

I buy a car magazine, a football magazine, a comic and a music magazine every week. I don't save much, maybe a pound.

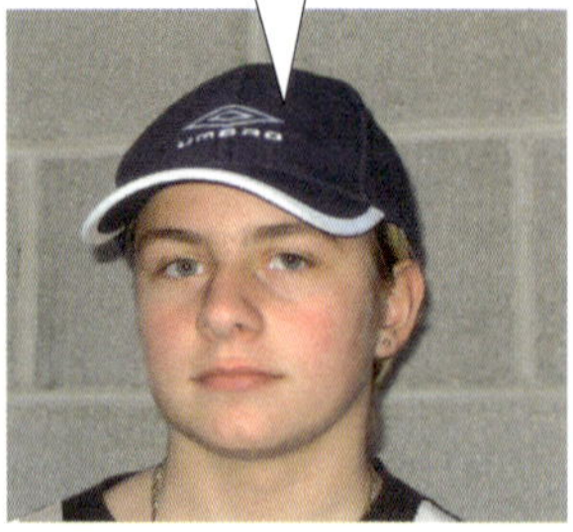

Tim

Lucy *doesn't buy many magazines.* Florian ________________________________

than Lucy, but Tim ________________________________.

2010 2011 Florian *saves* ________________ than Tim, but Lucy ________________.

11 PRONUNCIATION Stress (Betonung) ▸ p. 29 8

*Is the stress in the same place in German and in English? Write **Y** (= Yes) or **N** (= No).*

1	hamster	–	Hamster	Y	6	music	–	Musik	______
2	project	–	Projekt	N	7	judo	–	Judo	______
3	jacket	–	Jackett	______	8	problem	–	Problem	______
4	picnic	–	Picknick	______	9	photo	–	Foto	______
5	pullover	–	Pullover	______	10	person	–	Person	______

12 Compare (Comparison of adjectives) ▸ p. 30 • GF 4a/c–d (pp. 135–136)

*What do you think? Write sentences with ... **than** ...*

1

English, Maths (easy):

Maths is easier than English. / English is easier than Maths.

2

a fish, a hamster (nice):

____

3

tennis, table tennis (good):

____

4

a cat, a mouse (big):

____

5

spy stories, detective stories (scary):

____

2112

13 WRITING Millie, Minnie, Molly (Comparison of adjectives) ▸ p. 30 • GF 4a/c–d (pp. 135–136)

Compare Millie, Minnie and Molly Muddles. Write five sentences or more. Use: **young, old, big, small, long, short, dark, funny**

Ideas: Who is younger/bigger than the others? Who is the oldest? Who has got the longest hair, the darkest hair? Who is the funniest?

Millie, 4 Minnie, 2 Molly, 6

Millie is older than Minnie, but she's younger than Molly. Molly is the oldest and Minnie

2213

14 Which is the most exciting? (Comparison of adjectives) ▸ p. 31 • GF 4b–d (pp. 135–136)

What do you think? Write sentences.

1 exciting: A 

B  C 

I think B is the most exciting.

2 dangerous: A  B  C 

3 expensive: A  B  C 

4 interesting: A  B 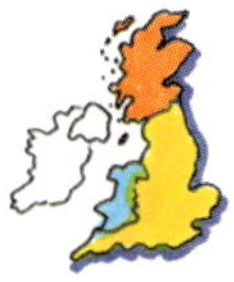 C 

2214

15 READING Dogs ▸ p. 31

a) *Read about the four dogs* **Sam**, **James**, **Boss** *and* **Pluto**. *Who's who? Write their names under the pictures.*

______________ ______________ ______________ ______________

Sam is the smallest dog, but he's got the longest hair and the longest ears. Boss is louder than all the other dogs. He makes lots of noise all the time – in the park, in the garden, in the house. The neighbours aren't very happy. James has got the biggest head and very short legs. He isn't as pretty as the others and he isn't as fast, but he's a very nice dog because he never makes problems. Pluto is the fastest of all the dogs. He's got the longest body and the longest legs. He can run for miles in the park – like the wind. One dog has got a long body with short hair and short legs. He looks really funny: like a sausage.

2315

b) *Match the dogs to the kids.*

Ali:

My dog is the fastest.
His name is ______________ .

Sue:

My dog is the smallest.
His name is ______________ .

Nick:

My dog is the loudest.
His name is ______________ .

Ed:

My dog is the slowest – and
he isn't the prettiest, but for me he's the greatest.
His name is ______________ .

Now you

Which dog do you like? Why? How is he different from the others? Write at least two sentences.

____

____

____

16 What do you think? (Comparison of adjectives)

▸ p. 31 • GF 4 (pp. 135–136)

Choose a word from each list and write sentences.

funny	DVD
good	*person*
bad	pop group
boring	comic
interesting	quiz show
difficult	computer game
exciting	book

1 The *funniest person* I know is ______.

2 The *worst* ______.

3 The ______.

4 ______

5 ______

6 ______

7 ______

17 WORDS Opposites

▸ p. 31

Which of Prunella's plates go together? Match, colour and write pairs of opposites.

start – finish

______

______

18 WORDS You can see films here ▸ p. 31

Complete the puzzle. ▸ *What's the word in the green boxes?*

1 You can see films here.	1				c	___	___	___	___	___	
2 The opposite of 'expensive' is ...	2			___	___	___	___	___			
3 Another word for 'terrible' is ...	3				___	___	___	___	___		
4 Jack has money ...	4			___	___	___	___	___	___	___	s
5 Jack needs a new ... of trainers.	5		___	___	___	___					
6 Prunella: What's the ..., Sophie?	6		___	___	___	___	___	___			
7 When you can use paper again, it's ...	7	___	___	___	___	___	___	___	___		

You can buy cheap things here: ▸ ____________________ shop.

19 MEDIATION Shopping for trainers ▸ p. 31 • SF (p. 131)

Florian is in a shoe shop in Bristol with his German cousin Heike.

Heike Sag der Verkäuferin, ich brauche ein Paar neue Turnschuhe. Sie können billig sein.

Florian Excuse me, she needs a new pair ____________________.

Shop assistant Ask her what size and what colour she would like. We have got a lot of new models.

Florian ____________________

Heike Ich bin nicht sicher. Sag ihr, ich möchte einige anprobieren. Sie haben schöne Schuhe.

Florian ____________________

Shop assistant What about blue? We have got some nice new models in pink too. But they're expensive. Maybe she doesn't want to spend so much money on trainers.

Florian ____________________

____

Shop assistant She can try on these. They're really nice. It's the last pair in this colour.

Florian ____________________

Heike Sie passen nicht. Sie sind viel zu eng. Und sie sind ein bisschen zu teuer. Hat sie andere?

Florian ____________________

(Twenty minutes later.)
Florian Heike, komm jetzt. Du hast schon vierzehn Paar Turnschuhe anprobiert.
Heike Klar. Gehen wir. Ich habe sowieso nicht genug Geld.

20 WORKING WITH THE TEXT The Clothes Project ▸ pp. 38–39

a) *Read pp. 38–39 of your student's book again. What's right? Tick (✔) A, B or C.*

1 Sophie and Jack are working on the project at ☐ A school. ☐ B Jack's house. ☐ C Sophie's house.

2 When they talk about the project, Jack has ☐ A lots of ideas. ☐ B no ideas. ☐ C only one good idea.

3 Who had the idea for a fashion show? ☐ A Jack and Sophie. ☐ B Lesley and Ananda. ☐ C Rachel and Tom.

4 Who went upstairs and into the attic first? ☐ A Prunella. ☐ B Jack. ☐ C Sophie.

5 What did Prunella drop? ☐ A A plate and a hat. ☐ B A plate, a hat and a pair of shoes. ☐ C A plate, a hat and three pairs of shoes.

6 The dress from the wardrobe is ☐ A long and white. ☐ B short and blue. ☐ C long and blue.

b) *What goes together? Match and write under the correct pictures.*

Something scary • Tea first • Poor Grandma's plates • Up to the attic • What about a fashion show? • In Grandma's wardrobe

____

____

____

____

____

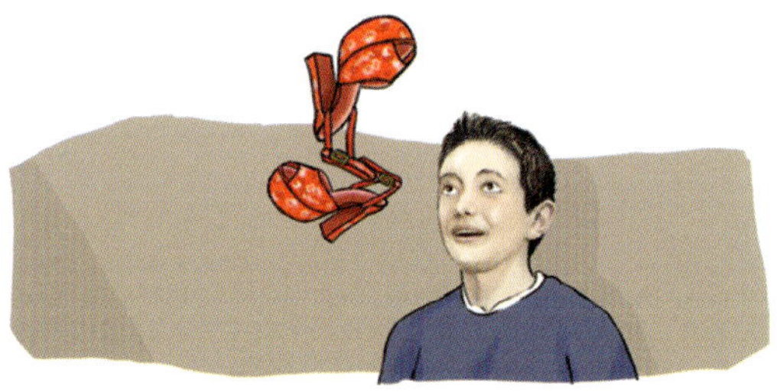

____

c) *Now retell the story in about eight sentences. Use the simple past and write in your exercise book.*

1 Clothes: write the names.

1
2
3
4
5
6

2701

2 Find group words for these things.

1 English • Maths • Art • PE

2 cinema • shopping • computer games

3 hair • nose • eyes • ears

2702 4 dress • shorts • trousers • pullover

3 Complete with *mine*, *yours*, ...

1 *Tim* Is this old jacket ______ , Becky?

2 *Becky* No, it isn't ______ . Ask Mum. Maybe it's ______ . Or ask Dad.

2703 3 *Tim* Ask Dad? It isn't ______ . It's pink with little white rabbits!

4 Compare with *than*.

1 Art – Music: easy

2 detective stories – comics: exciting

3 Sophie – Emily: nice

4 the Simpsons – Mr Bean: funny

5 a summer holiday – a holiday in the snow: good

6 a boring Sunday – a long school day: bad

2704

20 points

Now you

2705 2706 *Write about shopping. What do you buy with your pocket money? Do you spend much money on sweets, drinks, magazines? What do you spend most money on? Do you save much?*
Write at least five sentences in your exercise book.

Jetzt kann ich …	**Sehr gut!**	**OK**	**Verbessern!**
HÖREN: Ich kann …			
… die Arbeitsanweisungen, Fragen und Erklärungen meiner Lehrerin/meines Lehrers verstehen.	☐	☐	☐
… verstehen, was im Unterricht von meinen Mitschülern/-innen gesagt, gefragt und gespielt wird.	☐	☐	☐
… das Wichtigste aus Hörtexten der Units Welcome back, 1 und 2 meines Buchs sowie die Listening-Aufgaben meines Workbooks verstehen.	☐	☐	☐
… die Vokabeln der Units Welcome back, 1 und 2 verstehen.	☐	☐	☐
SPRECHEN: Ich kann …			
… im Unterricht frei erzählen und fragen, auch wenn ich kleine Fehler mache.	☐	☐	☐
… korrekt und flüssig die Wörter der Units Welcome back, 1 und 2 aussprechen und anwenden.	☐	☐	☐
… mich an Rollenspielen und an gespielten Szenen aus meinem Buch beteiligen.	☐	☐	☐
… über das Wetter sprechen.	☐	☐	☐
… mit dem *simple past* sagen, was ich gestern/letzte Woche/in den Ferien getan habe und wo ich gewesen bin.	☐	☐	☐
… über Geld, Taschengeld, Einkäufe, das Ausgeben und Sparen von Geld sprechen.	☐	☐	☐
… die Vokallaute [ɜː], [ɪə] und [eə] voneinander unterscheiden und richtig aussprechen.	☐	☐	☐
LESEN: Ich kann …			
… eine Postkarte oder einen kurzen Brief auf Englisch lesen und verstehen.	☐	☐	☐
… eine Karte von Europa verstehen.	☐	☐	☐
… die längeren Erzähltexte und Dialoge der Units Welcome back, 1 und 2 lesen und verstehen.	☐	☐	☐
… die längeren Erzähltexte und Dialoge der Units Welcome back, 1 und 2 ohne Probleme laut vorlesen.	☐	☐	☐
… kurze Sachtexte verstehen.	☐	☐	☐
SCHREIBEN: Ich kann …			
… eine Postkarte oder einen kurzen Brief an Freunde oder Verwandte schreiben.	☐	☐	☐
… Tagebucheinträge schreiben.	☐	☐	☐
… darüber schreiben, was ich in den Sommerferien gemacht habe.	☐	☐	☐
… die Wörter der Units Welcome back, 1 und 2 richtig schreiben.	☐	☐	☐
LAND UND LEUTE: Ich …			
… habe etwas über Cornwall und New York gelernt.	☐	☐	☐
… weiß, wie britische Schüler ihre Freizeit verbringen.	☐	☐	☐

Jetzt kann ich ...	Sehr gut!	OK	Verbessern!
GRAMMATIKVERSTÄNDNIS: Ich kann ...			
... die Verbformen des *simple present* (z.B. *play, make*) und des *simple past* (z.B. *played, made*) erkennen und voneinander unterscheiden.	☐	☐	☐
... mit dem *simple past* ausdrücken, was ich oder andere zu einem gewissen Zeitpunkt in der Vergangenheit gemacht haben (z.B. *Yesterday I worked/ saw/bought* ...).	☐	☐	☐
... mit *mine, yours, his* usw. ausdrücken, was jemandem gehört.	☐	☐	☐
... Dinge und Personen vergleichen. Dazu steigere ich Adjektive mit *-er/-est* oder mit *more/most* (z.B. *big, bigger, biggest, expensive, more expensive, most expensive*).	☐	☐	☐
VOKABELVERSTÄNDNIS: Ich kann ...			
... Wörter, die das Wetter beschreiben (z.B. *sunny, rainy, cloudy*), richtig verwenden.	☐	☐	☐
... viele Ländernamen (z.B. *Italy, Scotland, Wales*) richtig verwenden.	☐	☐	☐
... 'Ferien'-Wörter (z.B. *plane, fly, beach, sea, mountains, lake*) richtig verwenden.	☐	☐	☐
... Wörter für Kleidungstücke und Schuhe (z.B. *trousers, skirt, trainers*) richtig verwenden.	☐	☐	☐
... mehrere Präpositonen des Ortes (z.B. *behind, next to*) richtig verwenden.	☐	☐	☐
SKILLS – LERNEN UND ARBEITEN: Ich ...			
... kann Bilder beschreiben, indem ich sage, wo sich etwas genau befindet. Dazu verwende ich z.B. *in the middle/background/foreground*.	☐	☐	☐
... kann Wörter nach einem Oberbegriff in Gruppen sammeln und ordnen.	☐	☐	☐
... kann eine Mindmap erstellen, um Ideen zu sammeln und zu ordnen.	☐	☐	☐
... kann mit einem Partner oder einer Partnerin und in einer Gruppe arbeiten.	☐	☐	☐
... weiß, dass ich bei der Mediation nur das Wesentliche übersetzen und weitergeben muss.	☐	☐	☐

WAS ICH FÜR MEIN ENGLISCHLERNEN GETAN HABE: Ich habe ...	häufig	manchmal	nie
... am Unterrichtsgespräch aktiv teilgenommen.	☐	☐	☐
... ein Vokabelheft oder eine Vokabelkartei geführt.	☐	☐	☐
... mit Mindmaps Ideen gesammelt und geordnet.	☐	☐	☐
... mit dem Grammar File in meinem Buch gearbeitet.	☐	☐	☐
... mit dem Skills File in meinem Buch gearbeitet.	☐	☐	☐

WIE ICH MICH VERBESSERN KÖNNTE: Ich könnte ...

- ... den Unterrichtsstoff jeden Tag zu Hause kurz wiederholen. ☐
- ... Texte aus meinem Buch zu Hause laut lesen. ☐
- ... kurze Texte von der CD nachsprechen und auswendig lernen. ☐
- ... schwierige Wörter häufiger abschreiben. ☐
- ... mindestens ein Gedicht/einen Reim auswendig lernen. ☐
- ... das Grammar File und das Skills File mehr nutzen und die vorgeschlagenen Aufgaben bearbeiten. ☐

Unit 3 Animals in the city

1 WORDS Find the animals ▸ pp. 42–43

a) *Write the correct names of the animals.*

f x o	fox	p w e o c o k d r e	
r g o f		g h e h d g e o	
e r d e		r s u l r e q i	

3001
3002

b) *Find the animals. Write sentences with* on the right, on the left (of the picture), in the middle, at the top, at the bottom, in the background, …

1 There's a frog at the bottom on the left.

2 There's a ________________.

3 ________________

4 ________________

5 ________________

6 ________________

c) *Choose your favourite animal in a) and write three sentences about it in your exercise book.*
Ideas: My favourite animal is the … It's big/small/fast/slow/quiet/dangerous/… It lives in … It likes …

2 What will they need? (will-future) ▸ p. 44 • GF 5 (p. 137)

Tim and Florian want to go on a bike trip to a lake. The weather will be hot. What do you think they'll need? Write sentences with **They'll need …** *or* **They won't need …**

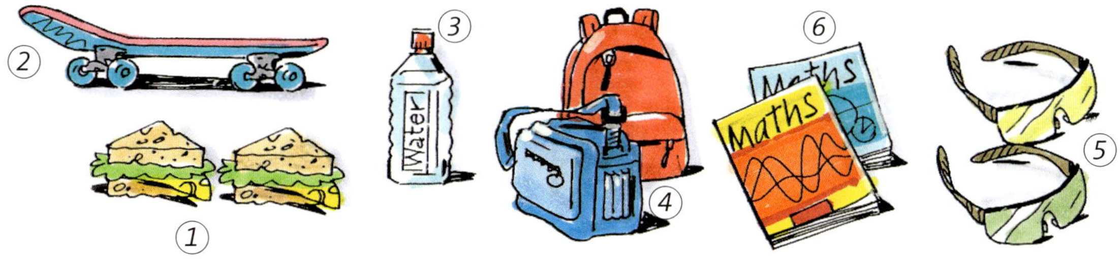

1 They'll need some sandwiches.

2 They won't need

3

4

5

3102 6

3 When will you be home? (will-future: questions) ▸ p. 44 • GF 5 (p. 137)

*Emily wants to go to a party. Her mum asks her some questions. Write the questions with a question word (***when***,* **how***,* **who***) +* **will***. Choose the correct verb:* **be***,* **finish***,* **get***,* **phone***,* **start***,* **take**

1 When will the party start? – At about seven o'clock, I think.

2 How many kids – About fifteen kids will be there.

3 – Not later than ten or ten-thirty.

4 home? – By train, with three of the other girls.

5 – Gemma's dad will take us to the station.

3103 3104 6 – I'll phone when we get on the train.

Now you

How old will you be on your next birthday? Do you think you'll have a party? How many friends will you invite? What will you have to eat? Will you play games? Write at least five sentences in your exercise book: **I think I'll …***,* **I/We probably won't …**

4 Baby hedgehogs (Conditional sentences) ▸ p. 45 • GF 6 (p. 138)

*If you find a baby hedgehog, what will you do? Write sentences with **I'll** (**I will**).*

1 give

2 be/careful

3 keep/warm

4 feed/with cat food

If I find a baby hedgehog, ...

1 *I'll give it water.* ______ 3 ______

3204 2 ______ 4 ______

5 Extra Tim's mum always says ... (Conditional sentences) ▸ p. 45 • GF 6 (p. 138)

*Match the sentence parts. Then write sentences with **If** ...*

1 eat lots of sweets	be ill
2 talk in class	get bad teeth
3 go to bed late	be tired tomorrow
4 watch scary DVDs	have problems with your teachers
5 eat too many hamburgers	have bad dreams

1 *If you eat lots of sweets, you'll get bad teeth.*

2 ______

3 ______

4 ______

5 ______

6 Extra What will you do if ...? (Conditional sentences) ▸ p. 45 • GF 6 (p. 138)

*Complete the sentences with **I'll**/**we'll** + a verb or with the simple present.*
Use the ideas in brackets ( ) or your own ideas.

1 If the weather is good on Saturday, I *'ll go to the park. / 'll go to the shops.* (park)

2 If my friend comes this afternoon, we ______.(DVDs)

3 I'll buy a CD next week if ______.(enough money)

4 I'll go to my friend's party if ______.(an invitation)

7 WORDS A puzzle ▸ p. 45

Write the answers in the puzzle. ▸ *Then find the new word in the orange boxes.*

1 Foxes and squirrels are … animals.
2 … are really pretty animals.
3 Ananda found two hedgehog …
4 The opposite of 'outside' is …
5 If you give hedgehogs milk, they get …
6 Keep them warm with a hot-water …
7 Don't give hedgehog babies milk or …

1	2	3	4	5	6	7
		a	n			
	r				l	
d						

▸ You can find lots about animals on the RSPCA ______________.

8 REVISION Animals (Comparison of adjectives) ▸ p. 45 • GF 4 (pp. 135–136)

*Compare the animals. Write sentences with … **than** …*

1  (big) *A hedgehog is bigger than a hamster.*

2  (boring) ______________

3  (pretty) ______________

4  (interesting) ______________

5  (scary) ______________

3308

9 READING Tim's problem ▸ p. 45

a) *Tim is telling Lucy about a problem. Read about the problem.*

I've got a friend in the next village. His name is Benny. His birthday is on Thursday and I've got an invitation to his party.
I would really like to go because after the party there's a junior disco. But there's a problem. It isn't easy to get to Benny's house. His parents have a nice house with a big garden, but it's at the end of the village. I'll have to go there by bus, because my dad can't take me on that day, and there aren't many buses to the village. I'll have to come home by bus because my dad won't be in Bristol. He'll be in London.
And there's another problem. The last bus from Benny's village goes at 9.30, and the junior disco won't finish before 10 o'clock. If I stay till the end, I won't get the last bus. And I'll have to walk to the bus alone, and it will be dark.
Mum doesn't think that's a good idea. All Benny's friends want to stay till the end of the disco because they don't live far away. Benny says I can stay the night at his house, but how will I get to school the next morning? I'll have to get up very early. If I don't get the bus, I'll get to school too late for the first lesson. My French teacher will be cross again, and I'll have to do extra homework. Then my friends will go to the cinema without me. I don't know what to do.

b) *Right or wrong? Tick (✔) the correct box.*

	Right	Wrong
1 Tim has got an invitation to Benny's party.	☐	☐
2 Benny's parents have a nice house with a garden in Bristol.	☐	☐
3 Tim's dad can take him to Benny's house.	☐	☐
4 If Tim stays to the end of the party, he'll get the last bus home.	☐	☐
5 If he doesn't get the last bus, he'll have to stay the night at Benny's house.	☐	☐
6 If he stays at Benny's house, he won't have to get up early.	☐	☐
7 He won't be late for school on the next day.	☐	☐
8 If Tim is late for school, the teacher will give him extra homework.	☐	☐
9 If Tim gets extra homework, he'll have to stay at home in the evening.	☐	☐
10 If he has to stay at home, his friends won't go to the cinema.	☐	☐

● ***c)*** **Extra** *What will happen if ...? Write four sentences with If ... about Tim's problem in your exercise book.*

If Tim goes to the party, he'll have to go there by bus.

10 WRITING Korky

▸ p. 45

a) Your dog Korky is ill. Write an e-mail about Korky to a friend. Link two sentences with a ***red*** *or a* ***blue*** *word.*

When After	My dog Korky is eleven years old. I'm not very happy today. He always eats his food. I come home from school. I took him to the park yesterday. I feed him. He's always a happy dog. We're very sad.	but and because so	He's my best friend. Korky is ill. He doesn't want it now. We usually go to the park. He just sat under a tree. He usually wants to play with me. He's very quiet now. Maybe we'll send an e-mail to the Animal Hotline.

Dear

My dog Korky is eleven years old and he's my best friend.

I'm not very happy today

3510

b) Now write three more sentences about Korky. Use a red or a blue word from a) in each sentence.

11 At school (Adverbs of manner) ▸ p. 46 • GF 7a–b, d (p. 139)

Adjective or adverb? Cross out (✕) the wrong word.

The Bristol kids like school and they're good students too. Sophie usually works (~~careful~~/carefully) and her work isn't (bad/badly). Ananda learns (quick/quickly) and works (quietly/quiet). Most of the boys learn (easily/easy) too, but sometimes they are really (horrible/horribly). Mr Kingsley is always (nicely/nice) to his students, but when they talk (loud/loudly) he's sometimes (angry/angrily). When he gives the students extra homework, they are suddenly (quiet/quietly) – and not very (happy/happily).

3611

12 How? (Adverbs of manner) ▸ p. 46 • GF 7a–b, d (p. 139)

What are the Muddles' kids doing now, and how? Complete the sentences with adverbs.
Choose from: **angrily, dangerously, loudly, quickly, terribly**

1

2

3

4

1 Max is eating quickly.

2 Molly is riding her bike ______.

3 Mr Muddles is shouting ______.

4 Micky is laughing ______

5 Maggie is dancing ______.

6 Millie is running ______.

5

6

Now you

How do you do these things? Write sentences with an adverb.
1 *eat your breakfast* 2 *ride your bike* 3 *dance* 4 *talk* 5 *sing* 6 *paint*

13 Find the word (Adverbs of manner) ▸ p. 47 • GF 7 (p. 139)

Write the adverbs in the puzzle and find the new word in the green boxes.

badly	easily	fast	hard	slowly	well

1 Jo loves football. He can run very …

2 Sophie is in the Dance Club. She dances very …

3 Ananda is good at school. She works very …

4 Jack writes stories. He can write them …

5 But Jack hates sports. He plays football …

6 Jo doesn't like Maths. He works too …

				▼				
1	_	_	_	_				
2			_	_	_	_		
3		_	_	_	_			
				r				
4	_	_	_	_	_	_		
5				_	_	_	_	_
6			_	_	_	_	_	_
				y				

▸ Polly sings ______________ .

Now you

What do you usually do well? What do you often do fast? What do you always do carefully? Write three sentences.

Just for fun

What goes up very slowly and comes down very fast?[1]

____

____

____

14 WORDS The odd one out ▸ p. 47

Find the odd one out. Then look at the number in brackets ( ) and write the letter of the word. Make a word from these letters.

1 mountains lake trees ~~view~~ sea	view	(3)	e
2 shirt trousers face jeans jacket	______	(4)	___
3 fox deer squirrel budgie mole	______	(4)	___
4 car bike station plane train	______	(6)	___
5 church rubbish library museum school	______	(7)	___
6 stormy foggy rainy badly cloudy	______	(3)	___
7 horrible awful terrible amazing	______	(7)	___
8 hamster tortoise rabbit guinea pig hutch	______	(1)	___

▸ Sleepy is slow, but very sweet. He's a ______________ .

[1] An elephant in a lift.

15 STUDY SKILLS Scanning ▸ p. 47 • SF (p. 126)

What do you know about red deer? Read the questions below, then scan the text to find the answers as quickly as you can. Write down your answers.

Description
The red deer is the biggest wild animal in the UK. In summer they are dark red or brown. In winter they are dark brown or grey. They can swim well.

How long do they live?
Deer usually live as long as ten or fifteen years. Deer in parks can live for twenty years.

Their enemies
Many young deer survive only for a few weeks because the weather is too cold for them. Sometimes foxes and wild cats kill deer babies for food. But life is dangerous for older animals too. Every year cars kill about 40,000 deer on the roads.

Where do they live?
About 350,000 red deer live wild in Scotland. They live on the islands near Scotland too. You can see them in many places, in parks and even in the mountains. They like to live near lots of trees, because they can find more food there. They usually live in groups of 10 to[1] 40 animals, but sometimes there are more than a hundred deer in one group.

Baby deer
A deer mother usually has one baby every year, in May or June. A baby deer is brown and white. It can stand after only a few minutes and can run after a few hours. A young deer stays with its mother till she has another baby.

Did you know?
A wild fox lives about seven years. A fox in a zoo lives 14 years. And: Foxes can swim!

1 What colour are deer in summer? __________

2 Can deer swim? __________

3 How long do deer usually live? __________

4 Deer have enemies. What or who are they? __________

5 How many deer live in Scotland? __________

6 How many babies does a mother have every year? __________

7 How soon can a baby deer run? __________

[1] to [tə] hier: *bis*

16 PRONUNCIATION [f] – [v] – [w] ▸ p. 47 🎧 9

a) *Listen and say the words. Do you hear [f], [v] or [w]? Tick (✔) the right box. Then write the word.*

	1 [f]	2 [v]	3 [w]			1 [f]	2 [v]	3 [w]	
1	☐	☐	✔	water	5	☐	☐	☐	______
2	☐	☐	☐	______	6	☐	☐	☐	______
3	☐	☐	☐	______	7	☐	☐	☐	______
3916 4	☐	☐	☐	______	8	☐	☐	☐	______

Count your points: [f] = 1, [v] = 2, [w] = 3. If your answers are correct, you will have 16 points!

b) *Now say these sentences as quickly as you can.*

1 On a foggy Friday in November Fred found fifty-five frogs in the fridge.
2 Last week we visited a family in a very funny village in Wales.
3 When Will visited Vicky and Val the weather was very windy.

17 WORDS Animals ▸ p. 47

a) *Find the animal names. Tick (✔) the letters, then write the name and match it with a picture.*

1 b k e a a n r g — bear
2 a m o r n k o e y — ______
3 o l i c o r n o — ______
4 h c i p o p d o i — ______
5 e l e l p h e a c n a t — ______
6 r m h e i l n o — ______

b) *With the extra letters in a) 1–6, find and write the names of three more animals.*

1 ______
2 ______
3917 3 ______

Did you know?
A hippo can run faster than a man.

18 LISTENING A walk in the woods[1] ▸ p. 47 10

a) Mr Baxter is walking in the woods with Tim and Becky. Listen carefully.

*b) Now tick (✓) the correct answer, **A**, **B** or **C**. Sometimes more than one answer is correct.*

1 Tim is talking …	A	quietly.	B	loudly.	C	quickly.
2 There's a programme on TV tonight about …	A	moles.	B	deer.	C	squirrels.
3 What did Becky see last year?	A	A fox.	B	A deer.	C	Two deer.
4 Why does a woodpecker make a hole[2] in a tree?	A	To sleep in.	B	To put food in.	C	To lay eggs[3] in.
5 A fast red fox can run … miles an hour.	A	13	B	30	C	33
6 What do foxes eat?	A	Mice.	B	Cats.	C	Fruit.
7 What does Becky see in a tree?	A	A red squirrel.	B	A mole.	C	A woodpecker.
8 Tim says, '… are cool.'	A	Frogs	B	Hedgehogs	C	Moles
9 Becky likes …	A	deer.	B	frogs.	C	hedgehogs.
10 Tim wants to take frogs home and put them …	A	in the garden.	B	in a fish bowl.	C	in a cage.

4018

[1] woods [wʊdz] *Wald* [2] hole [həʊl] *Loch* [3] lay eggs [leɪ egz] *Eier legen*

1 What is it?

1 a __________ 4 __________

2 __________ 5 __________

3 __________ 6 __________

4101

2 What will the weather be like?

*Look at the picture. Complete with **'ll (will)** and **won't**.*

1 In England it ____ ____ be sunny and it ________ rain.

4102 *2* In Scotland it ____ ____ rain, but it ________ be cold.

3 What will happen if ...?

Complete with the simple present or the will-future.

1 If I __________ (find) a hedgehog baby, I __________ (have to) give it water.

2 It __________ (get ill) if I __________ (give) it milk.

4103 *3* If I __________ (give) it cat food, it __________ (survive).

4 Describe the pictures.

How? Use adverb forms of:

careful	quick	quiet	angry

1 Dan is running __________.

2 Sophie is riding her bike __________.

3 Ananda is working __________.

4104 *4* Mr Kingsley is shouting __________.

20 points

Now you

*In your exercise book, write about your future with **will ('ll)** and **won't**. Ideas: **live in Germany/on the moon/ under the sea**, **have a good job**, **have a car/plane**, **speak very good English***

4105
4106 *When I'm 25, I think I'll ...*

Unit 4 A weekend in Wales

1 WORDS Town and country

▸ pp. 58–59

Find the mistakes in the lists. Cross out the wrong words and write them in the correct list.

In town		In the country	
~~valley~~	traffic	sheep	valley
forest		~~traffic~~	
sports centre		train station	
field		cow	
hill		factory	
farm		cinema	
animals		park	
		DVD shop	

4201

2 LISTENING Last weekend

▸ p. 58–59 11

Tim and Florian are talking about what they did at the weekend. First, listen to the dialogue. Which **town** *words do you hear? Which* **country** *words do you hear? Listen again and make two lists.*

Town words	Country words
station	farm

4202

3 Where and when (Word order: place before time) ▸ p. 60 • GF 8b (p. 141)

Where will they be on Saturday?

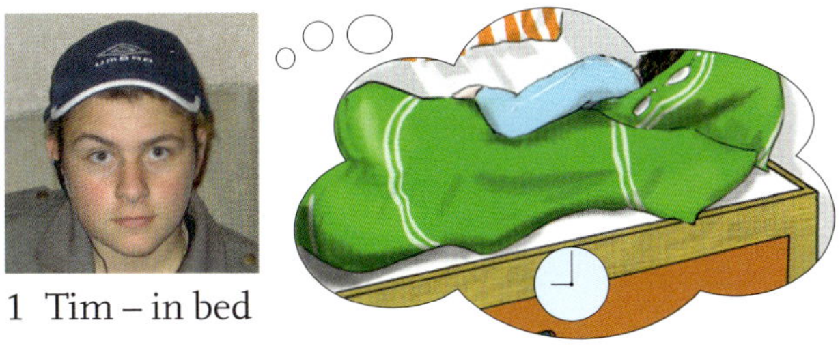
1 Tim – in bed

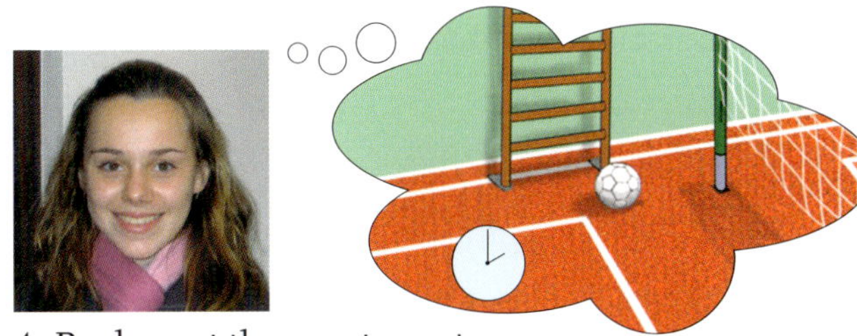
4 Becky – at the sports centre

2 Florian – at the bike shop

5 Becky and Tim – at a party

3 Becky and Lucy –at the shopping centre

6 Lucy and Florian – at the cinema

1 Tim *will be in bed at nine o'clock.*

2 Florian ______________________________.

3 Becky and Lucy ______________________________.

4 Becky ______________________________.

5 Becky and Tim ______________________________.

4303 *6* Lucy and Florian ______________________________.

Now you

Where will your mother/father/sister/brother/best friend/ ... probably be next week on Monday, on Saturday or on Sunday? Write at least three sentences.
Ideas: at home, at school, at a birthday party, in town, at a friend's house

My sister will be at school on Monday.

____

____

____

4 STUDY SKILLS Topic sentence ▸ p. 60 • SF (p. 129)

Jo is writing an essay about Wales, but he has got a computer virus[1]. In each paragraph his sentences are in the wrong order. Mark the topic sentence in each paragraph and write Jo's sentences in the correct order.

1 Lots of people visit the country every year too. Wales is only a small country. About 3 million people live there.

2 Over 320,000 people live there. Cardiff is the biggest city in Wales, with the most people. There are lots of interesting museums and a castle in the city centre.

3 It has got mountains, valleys and beaches. Wales is a beautiful country too. You can climb the mountains, ride your bike through the valleys or swim in the sea.

4 It's 1,190 metres. Don't go up it if you don't like walking. Snowdon is the biggest mountain in England and Wales.

1 Wales is only a small country. ____________________

____

2 ____________________

____

____

3 ____________________

____

____

4 ____________________

____

____

Did you know?

A village in Wales has a place name with 58 letters. Look!

'Llanfairpwllgwyngyllgogery-chwyrndrobwll Llantysiliogogogoch.'[2]

But people just say 'Llanfair PG'!

[1] virus ['vaɪrəs]
[2] You can hear the name at: www.EnglishG.de. Write this web-code: EG21WB44.

Activity page 1

Words in groups Unit 2

- *Colour the picture cards and cut them out. Then cut out the word cards.*
- *Put the picture cards and the word cards in 3 groups.*
- *On a piece of A4 paper or card, make 3 lists.*
- *Write a group word at the top of each list.*
- *Glue the pictures in the correct lists and glue the correct word cards next to the pictures.*
- *On the empty cards draw 3 more pictures and write 3 more words, one for each list.*

trousers	**skirt**	**ice cream**	**baseball cap**	
sweets	**cinema tickets**	**chips**	**comics**	
CDs and DVDs	**trainers**	**crisps**	**magazines**	

Activity page 2

A puzzle

Unit 4

- *Find the right verb forms.*
- *Cut out the cards in box 2 and complete box 1.*

box 1

go			take		
do			eat		
sing			wear		
give			choose		

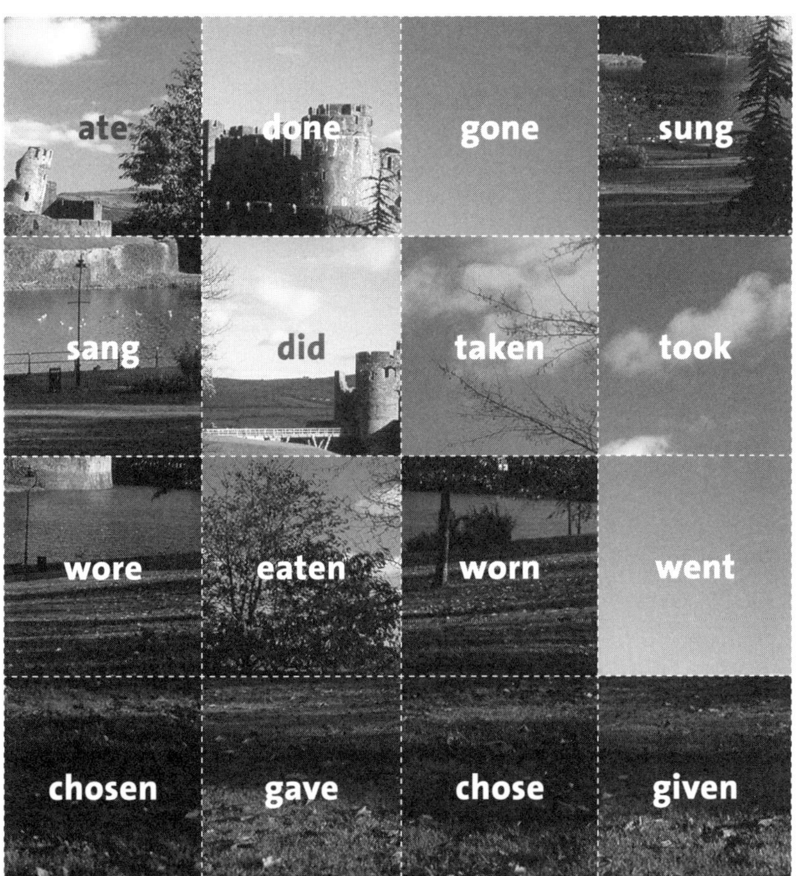

ate	done	gone	sung
sang	did	taken	took
wore	eaten	worn	went
chosen	gave	chose	given

box 2

Activity page 3

Memory game: town and country Unit 6

- *Cut out the word cards and the pictures.*
- *Put the cards on the table, so that you can't see the words and the pictures.*
- *Take two cards and match the correct picture and the word card. Go on!*
- *You can play this game with a partner.*

forest

river

ice rink

factory

market

pub

hills

valley

fields

supermarket

department store

police station

railway

traffic

post office

Activity page 4

A Valentine's Day[1] card

- *Cut out the Valentine's Day card and cut out the three sides of the little window.*
- *Cut out the picture of the bear. Put glue on the sides.*
- *Glue the picture of the bear in the window.*
- *Cut out 'Happy Valentine's Day'. Put the words at the top of the card.*
- *Colour the card.*

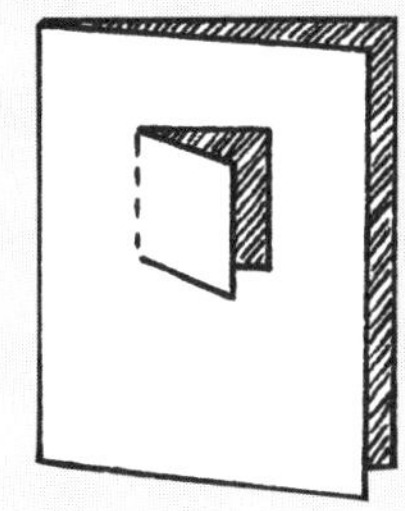

[1] *Valentine's Day* ['væləntaɪnz deɪ] *Valentinstag*

5 Dan has called his dad (Present perfect: regular verbs) ► p. 61 • GF 9, 10a–b (pp. 142–143)

Find and mark the regular verbs. Choose the correct verb and use it in the present perfect to write a sentence under each picture. Then match and add a sentence from the yellow box.

call take do prepare find go paint
eat tidy see drop come wash

It smells great. • Now Mr Shaw is happy. • Now they're clean too. • Poor Barnabas! • Now his mum will be happy. • Now their jeans are red and green too.

1 Dan – dad

Dan has called his dad.

Now Mr Shaw is happy.

2 Grandma – some Welsh soup

3 Tim and Florian – their skateboards

4 Tim – his ice cream

5 Sophie and Toby – Sheeba

6 Tim – his room

6 Find the forms (Past participles: irregular verbs) ▸ p. 61 • GF 10a (p. 142)

Find the missing past participles in the snake and complete the lists.

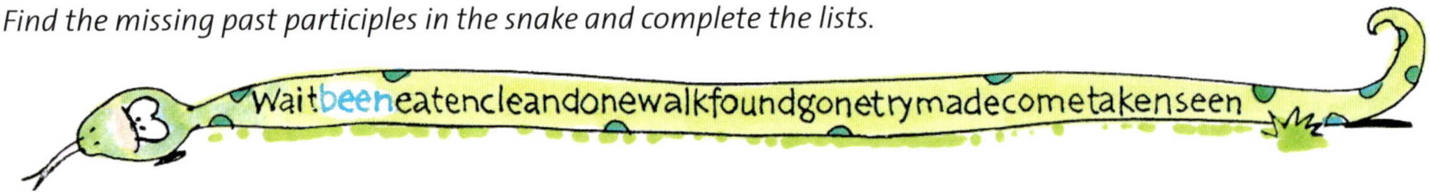

be – was – *been*	see – saw – ______	take – took – ______
go – went – ______	find – found – ______	do – did – ______
eat – ate – ______	make – made – ______	come – came – ______

4606

7 Monday morning at the Muddles' (Present perfect: already, not ... yet) ▸ p. 61 • GF 11 (p. 144)

What have the Muddles already done? What haven't they done yet? Write a sentence under each picture. Use the present perfect with **already** *or* **not ... yet**.

have a shower | do his homework | take out the rubbish | *make their beds* | go to school | eat their breakfast

1 Max *has already had a shower.*

2 Molly and Micky *haven't made their beds yet.*

3 Mr Muddles ______________________________.

4 Maggie and Minnie ______________________________.

5 Molly and Micky ______________________________.

6 Max ______________________________.

4607

Now you

What have you already done today? What haven't you done yet?
Write at least four sentences in your exercise book.

I've already had lunch. I haven't phoned my friends yet.

8 Jack has just ... (Present perfect: just) ▸ p. 61 • GF 11 (p. 144)

What have they just done? Complete the sentences. Use a verb from the list in the present perfect and just.

clean	*eat*	make	pack	see

① 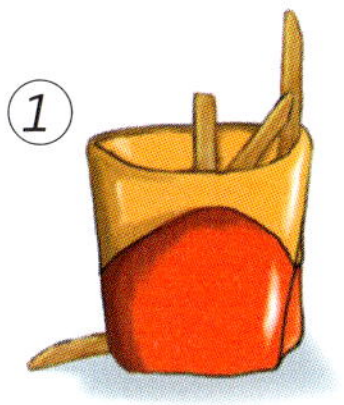
② 
③ 
④ 
⑤ 

1 Jack doesn't want any dinner. He *has just eaten some chips.*

2 Ananda is ready for the hockey match. She ______________________.

3 It smells good in the kitchen. Sophie ______________________.

4 Emily and her friend are nervous. They ______________________.

4708 5 The Thompsons are planning a trip. Grandpa ______________________.

9 WORDS Body words ▸ p. 62

***a)** Write the answers in the puzzle.*

1 You smell with this.

2 You have 32 of these.

3 You have ten of these.

4 You talk and eat with this.

5 We've got two arms and two ...

6 You think with this.

7 This starts with a 'k' – but you don't hear it.

4709 8 An elephant has very big ones.

1			_	_	_	_		
2	_	_	_	_	_			
3				_	_	_	s	
4			_	_	_	_	_	
5					_	_	_	s
6		_	_	_	_			
7			_	_	_	_		
8			_	_	_	s		

***b)** What's the word in the green boxes?*

Tim has played football with his friends.

▸ Now his ______________ hurts.

***c)** Tim tells his mum. Write a short dialogue in your exercise book. Use ideas from your student's book, p. 62.*

Mum: What's the matter, Tim?
Tim: I ...

Just for fun

Hello, Ed. What's the matter with you? Ah. You can't talk. I know! You have a sore throat.

10 Have they ever ...? (Present perfect: questions with ever)

▸ p. 63 • GF 10c, 11 (pp. 143–144)

Look at the pictures and write questions. Then write short answers.
Use: **been** (2x), **seen**, **found**, **played**, **eaten**

1 

✓

Q: *Has Ananda ever been to* ______ New York?

A: Yes, ______.

2 

✗

Q: Has ______.

A: ______

3 

✓

Q: Have the twins ______?

A: ______

4 

✗

Q: ______

A: ______

5 

✓

Q: ______

4810 A: ______

6 

✗

Q: ______ Toby and Emily ______?

A: ______

11 Extra REVISION The football match (Conditional sentences)

▸ p. 63 • GF 6 (p. 138)

Fill in the correct forms.

Dan It's the big match on Saturday. If Ed's knee still *hurts* (hurt), he *won't play* (play) in the team. That will be terrible.

Jo Right. If he *doesn't feel* (feel) better, his mum ______ (say) he can't play.

Dan If he ______ (play), who ______ (play) for him? Sam?

Jo Yes, Sam. But he isn't as good as Ed. If our team ______ (play) badly, Mr Kingsley ______ (be) very happy.

Dan I know. If we ______ (lose) another match, we ______ (be) the champions this year.

4811 *Jo* Right. If we ______ (win), the team ______ (be) really sad. And if I ______ (play) badly, Dad ______ (buy) me a new football.

12 READING … ▸ p. 63

a) *Read the story.*

Three years ago the Baxters visited a castle in Wales. Becky can remember the visit very well …
'It was a great visit,' said Tim. 'It was very funny too!' '*You* thought it was funny. But it was horrible for me,' said Becky. Lucy wanted to know why the visit was so horrible.
'Well,' said Tim. 'When we looked round the castle, I stayed with Mum and Dad, but Becky wanted to explore alone.'
'Be quiet!' said Becky angrily. 'I can tell Lucy the story.'
'Is it exciting?' asked Lucy with big eyes.
'Go on. Tell me about it!'
'Well, you see,' said Becky 'there was a tower, and in the tower I went up some stairs. I found a little door. Of course I wanted to know what was behind it, so I opened it and went inside. But it was windy, and – bang! The door closed behind me. I was alone in the dark. I shouted and shouted. I shouted so loudly that I had a sore throat, but nobody came.
Then suddenly I heard a noise behind me. Something moved. I felt really scared.'
'Wow! Well, go on, what was it? Something horrible?' Lucy wanted to know. 'How exciting!'
'I don't know. It was very dark in the room – and cold too. Just awful,' said Becky.
'Well, the castle is very old, and I think maybe there were a few very old dead bodies in there. Or maybe there was a cold, dangerous animal – a crocodile, a big snake or …,' said Tim.
'Don't be silly, Tim. I'm sure it was just a mouse,' Lucy went on. 'Well, what happened then?'
'Now it's my turn,' said Tim. 'Listen carefully. This is the best part of the story. Well, we didn't know where Becky was. But Mum and Dad didn't worry because Becky is always careful. But when we went in the tower I heard a noise. I thought it was an animal, so I explored …

4912

b) *Find the best title for the story:*

A A great castle B A scary story C A nice day out

c) *What's right? Tick (✔) A, B or C.*

	A	B	C
1 The Baxters visited a castle in	Wales.	England.	Scotland.
2 They went there	last year.	two years ago.	three years ago.
3 Becky thought the visit was	funny.	horrible.	exciting.
4 Lucy thought the story was	boring.	stupid.	exciting.
5 Becky was in the tower	alone.	with her parents.	with Tim.
6 In the room it was	dark and hot.	cold and dark.	hot and windy.

13 WRITING The end of the story ▸ p. 63

*Read the story in exercise **12** again and complete it. You can use these words or your own ideas.*

open • find • shout • happy • brother • laugh • save Becky's life • mouse

Tim went on, 'And then I saw the door. I…

____

____

____

____

____

____

14 WORDS My first is in … ▸ p. 63

***a)** What am I?*

1 My first is in	page	but not in	cage	p
2 My second is in	ate	but not in	pet	____
3 My third is in	tree	but not in	tea	____
4 My fourth is in	hear	but not in	here	____
5 My fifth is in	mad	but not in	dad	____
6 My sixth is in	men	but not in	man	____
7 My seventh is in	date	but not in	late	____
8 My eighth is in	said	but not in	sad	____
9 And my last is in	chair	but not in	hair	____

***b)** What's my name? It rhymes with **win**. If you know the answer, you can complete the sentence.*

My name is ____________ and I'm a ▸ ________________________.

15 WORDS Find the message ▸ p. 63

a) *Label the pictures.*

f a c t o r y (3)

(1)

(2)

(3)

(3)

(2)

(2)

(4)

(7)

(4)

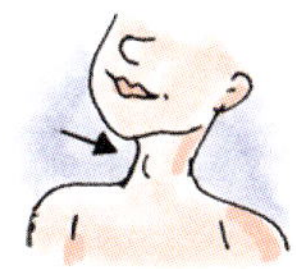
(3)

(3)

b) **Extra** *Find the letters in the green boxes, then write the message.*

The message is c ______________________________!

In English it means ______________________________!

16 PRONUNCIATION Stress in English and German (Betonung) ▸ p. 63 12

a) *Match and write correct words. Then write the German words. Listen to the words and mark the stress.*

		English	German
ca	nic	camel	Kamel
kang	mel		
temper	phant		
pic	aroo		
gar	over		
pull	age		
acc	ature		
ele	ent		

b) *One word has the same stress in English and German. Draw a ☺ next to it.*

17 WORDS Have you ever ... ▸ p. 63

a) Find the missing word in the blue box, write it down and then cross it out in the box.

1 Have you ... been to Australia? – No, never. *ever*

2 Look, I've ... a new CD. ______

3 If you feel very hot, maybe you have a ... ______

4 I've got a ... throat. It really hurts. ______

5 I don't feel well. I think I've got a ... ______

6 Tim hasn't ... Barnabas. He wants his food. ______

5217 7 If you don't clean your teeth you'll get a ... ______

TEMPERATUREWETOOTHACHELS~~EVER~~H
BOUGHTGFEDRASORENNCOLDY

b) Which letters are still in the blue box? Make two words.

Answer: ______

18 WORDS Pairs ▸ p. 63

Which words go together? Find and write pairs of opposites.

clever behind friend in front of
dirty love nobody *stupid* enemy lose
sad slow foreground somebody happy
background clean win hate fast

clever – *stupid* ______ – ______
______ – ______ ______ – ______
______ – ______ ______ – ______
______ – ______ ______ – ______
______ – ______ ______ – ______

1 What's in the picture?

1 ______

2 ______

3 ______

4 ______

5 ______

6 ______

5301

2 Write correct sentences.

1 I'll – at five-thirty – be – at the station.

______

______

2 We – till six – in the DVD shop – were.

______

______

5302

3 What have they done?

Use the present perfect of ***drop***, ***find***, ***make*** *and* ***pack*** *and complete the sentences.*

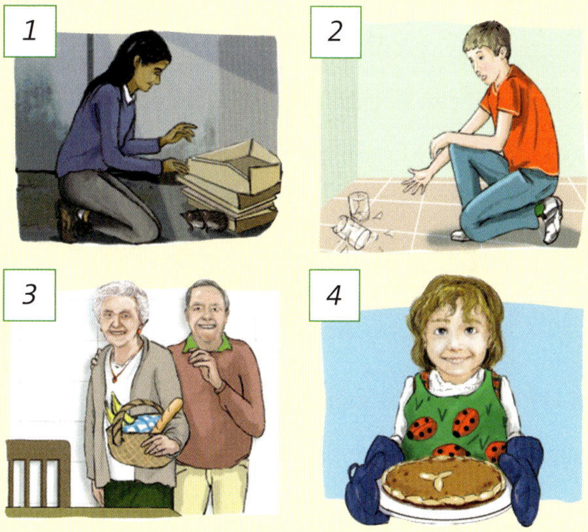

1 Ananda ______.

2 Jo ______.

3 The Thompsons ______.

5303 4 Emma ______.

4 Complete the words.

Mum Tim, what's the m ______? Are you feeling i ______?

Tim Yes, my throat h ______ and I have a t ______. And my head. I have a terrible h ______. And my legs hurt when I m ______. I can't go to school today.

5304 *Mum* Really? But the French test is today …

18 points

Now you

5305 5306 *In your exercise book, write three or four short paragraphs about your country. Start each paragraph with a topic sentence. You can use ideas from Jo's essay in exercise* ***4*** *(workbook, p. 44), or look at English websites about Germany for ideas. For example, try www.germany-tourism.de.*

Jetzt kann ich ...	**Sehr gut!**	**OK**	**Verbessern!**
HÖREN: Ich kann ...			
... die Anweisungen, Fragen und Erklärungen im Unterricht verstehen.	☐	☐	☐
... den Sinn einfacher Geschichten und Lieder auf CD verstehen.	☐	☐	☐
... eine längere Geschichte verstehen, auch wenn mir nicht alle Wörter bekannt sind.	☐	☐	☐
... verschiedene Akzente erkennen.	☐	☐	☐
... die Vokabeln der Units 3 und 4 verstehen.	☐	☐	☐
SPRECHEN: Ich kann ...			
... zu einem bestimmten Thema ein paar zusammenhängende Sätze frei sprechen, auch wenn ich kleine Fehler mache.	☐	☐	☐
... die Wörter der Units 3 und 4 richtig aussprechen und anwenden.	☐	☐	☐
... über Tiere im Wald und ihre Gewohnheiten sprechen.	☐	☐	☐
... sagen, was mir wehtut und andere fragen, was ihnen gesundheitlich fehlt.	☐	☐	☐
... die Konsonantenlaute [f], [v] und [w] voneinander unterscheiden und richtig aussprechen.	☐	☐	☐
LESEN: Ich kann ...			
... eine Postkarte oder einen kurzen Brief auf Englisch lesen und verstehen.	☐	☐	☐
... die längeren Erzähltexte und Dialoge der Units 3 und 4 lesen und verstehen.	☐	☐	☐
... die längeren Erzähltexte und Dialoge der Units 3 und 4 ohne Probleme laut vorlesen.	☐	☐	☐
... kurze Sachtexte lesen und verstehen.	☐	☐	☐
... Texte über Themen des Alltags lesen und verstehen, auch wenn mir nicht alle Wörter bekannt sind.	☐	☐	☐
SCHREIBEN: Ich kann ...			
... kurze und einfache E-Mails, Briefe oder Postkarten schreiben.	☐	☐	☐
... einfache Fragen zu den Texten der Units 3 und 4 schriftlich beantworten.	☐	☐	☐
... meine Sätze mit *time phrases* wie *first, then, after that, a few minutes later* miteinander verbinden. Dadurch klingen meine Texte interessanter.	☐	☐	☐
... meine Sätze mit *linking words* (z.B. *because, so, but*) miteinander verbinden, damit meine Texte flüssiger klingen.	☐	☐	☐
... die Wörter der Units 3 und 4 richtig schreiben.	☐	☐	☐
LAND UND LEUTE: Ich ...			
... weiß etwas über den britischen Tierverein RSPCA.	☐	☐	☐
... habe etwas über Wales und über die walisische Sprache gelernt.	☐	☐	☐

Jetzt kann ich ...	Sehr gut!	OK	Verbessern!
GRAMMATIKVERSTÄNDNIS: Ich kann ...			
... mit *will/won't* + Infinitiv (*will-future*) über die Zukunft sprechen und Vorhersagen machen (z.B. *I'll be* 14 *next year*).	☐	☐	☐
... mit einem *Conditional sentence* (*type 1*) ausdrücken, was unter bestimmten Bedingungen geschehen wird (z.B. *If you give a hedgehog water, it'll be happy*).	☐	☐	☐
... mit Adverbien der Art und Weise beschreiben, wie jemand etwas macht oder sagt. Adverbien bilde ich, indem ich *-ly* an das Adjektiv anhänge (z.B. *A hedgehog walks slowly*). Ich kenne auch die unregelmäßigen Adverbformen (z.B. *I work well/hard/fast*).	☐	☐	☐
... die Verbformen des *present perfect* erkennen und richtig bilden (z.B. *I have looked/been, he/she has looked/been*).	☐	☐	☐
... mit dem *present perfect* ausdrücken, was ich oder andere irgendwann in der Vergangenheit gemacht haben (z.B. *Jo has bought a new DVD*).	☐	☐	☐
VOKABELVERSTÄNDNIS: Ich kann ...			
... die Namen einiger Wild- und Zootiere (z.B. *squirrel, bear, lion*) richtig verwenden.	☐	☐	☐
... Wörter für Stadt und Land (z.B. *valley, field, forest, traffic*) richtig verwenden.	☐	☐	☐
... Wörter für Körperteile (z.B. *shoulder, stomach, ear, throat*) richtig verwenden.	☐	☐	☐
... Wörter für einige Krankheiten (z.B. *a cold, a toothache*) richtig verwenden.	☐	☐	☐
SKILLS – LERNEN UND ARBEITEN: Ich ...			
... kann in meinem Dictionary ein Wort ohne Probleme nachschlagen.	☐	☐	☐
... kann während des Hörens eines Hörtextes kurze Notizen dazu machen.	☐	☐	☐
... kann in einem langen Text nach Schlüsselwörtern suchen, um gezielte Informationen schnell zu finden. Im Englischen nennt man dies *scanning*.	☐	☐	☐
... weiß, dass ich in meinem Text einen Absatz mit einem *topic sentence* anfangen muss, der aussagt, worum es in dem Absatz geht.	☐	☐	☐

WAS ICH FÜR MEIN ENGLISCHLERNEN GETAN HABE: Ich habe ...	häufig	manchmal	nie
... ausprobiert, mit welchen Lern- und Arbeitstechniken ich am besten lernen und arbeiten kann.	☐	☐	☐
... die Aufgaben im Grammar File in meinem Buch bearbeitet.	☐	☐	☐
... die Aufgaben im Skills File in meinem Buch bearbeitet.	☐	☐	☐

WIE ICH MICH VERBESSERN KÖNNTE: Ich könnte ...

- ... am Unterricht aktiver teilnehmen. ☐
- ... neue und auch alte Vokabeln regelmäßig wiederholen. ☐
- ... nach jedem neuen Skills-Abschnitt in meinem Buch den dazugehörigen Abschnitt im Skills File aufmerksam lesen. ☐
- ... versuchen, bekannte Texte aus meinem Buch schriftlich und auch mündlich nachzuerzählen. ☐
- ... Übungen aus früheren Units in meinem Buch/ *Workbook* noch einmal durcharbeiten. ☐
- ... häufiger mit meiner CD arbeiten. ☐

Unit 5 Teamwork

1 WORDS Let's play the Bristol game! ▸ pp. 74–75

a) First, write the answers in the boxes.

1 You … at number one. — 1 s _ _ _ _

2 You need this to play. It has six numbers on it. — 2 _ _ _ _

3 Sometimes you have to move … — 3 _ _ _ _

4 Whose … is it? — 4 _ _ _ _

5 If you get to number 50 first, you … — 5 _ _ _

6 The game is about this city. — 6 _ _ _ _ _ _ _

b) Now make the name of a famous person from the letters in the green boxes.

5601 The name is ______________________ .

2 WORDS About Bristol ▸ pp. 74–75

Complete with the missing words from the boxes. Write them correctly.

3 ubp | 8 grsau | 10 wreTo | 4 dceols | 7 vSlsae | 2 bluit | 6 hcir | 5 kraMte | 9 btcooca | 1 negrenei

Brunel was a famous (1) engineer .

Brunel (2) ____________ the Temple Meads Station.

You can stop and look at this old pirate (3) ____________ .

You want to visit Cotham School, but it's (4) ____________ .

At St Nicholas (5) ____________ you can get a healthy snack.

Long ago, (6) ____________ people in Bristol had land in the Caribbean.

(7) ____________ helped them to grow (8) ____________ and (9) ____________ .

5602 In Bristol you can climb the famous Cabot (10) ____________ .

3 They're going to do a quiz (going to-future) ▸ p. 76 • GF 12 (p. 145)

Match and write sentence pairs.

Sophie wants two more students in her team. Sophie and Ananda want to win a prize. Jo has got a nice camera. The students need more details.	He She They	's/'re going to	make a brochure. *ask Jack and Dan.* find things out at the library. take the photos.

1 *Sophie wants two more students in her team. She's going to ask Jack and Dan.*

2 ______

3 ______

5703 4 ______

4 Extra What are the Muddles going to do? (going to-future) ▸ p. 76 • GF 12 (p. 145)

Write what they are going to do and what they aren't going to do this evening.

call friends • cook dinner • do • learn • play (2x) • wash • watch

1 Max:

Max is going to play the guitar.

He isn't ______

2 Micky and Molly:

______

______

3 Maggie:

______

______

4 Their mum and dad:

______

5704
5705 ______

Now you

What are you and your family or friends going to do this weekend?
Write a short paragraph in your exercise book.

I'm going to ... My sister/brother is going to ...

5 PRONUNCIATION Silent letters ▸ p. 76 13

Listen to the words and find the silent letters. Mark them in red. How many words with silent letters are there?

b u s i n e s s | w o u l d | i s l a n d
h a l f | h o u r | c a s t l e
c l i m b | s w i m | a n s w e r | W e d n e s d a y

5805

6 REVISION STUDY SKILLS (Learning words – Step 2) ▸ p. 77 • SF (p. 121)

a) *Find four group words and write them at the top of the lists. Write the other words in the correct groups. (Four words don't fit into a group.)*

animals | throat | body | market | bacon | paramedic | department store | policewoman | food | monkey | places | eggs | people | trousers | knee | soup | driver | engineer | lion | pie | bear | castle | cap | skirt | ear | hospital | shoulder | jacket | kangaroo

1 animals ____ 2 ____ 3 ____ 4 ____ 5 ____

b) *Four words in a) don't fit into the groups. Write them and find a group word for them.*

5806 1 ____ 2 ____ 3 ____ 4 ____ Group word: ____

7 REVISION What have they done? (Present perfect) ▸ p. 77 • GF 9–11 (pp. 142–144)

a) Find and mark the past participles. Then write them in the list.

s	b	h	f	o	u	n	d
h	e	a	r	d	c	n	w
v	e	d	s	b	s	l	r
y	n	b	l	y	e	j	i
e	a	t	e	n	e	d	t
g	p	q	k	v	n	o	t
k	l	m	w	g	o	n	e
j	n	c	t	a	k	e	n

▶	▼
found	*been*
___	___
___	___
___	___
___	___

b) Now complete with correct participles from a).

Sophie Have you already *been* ___ to the Georgian House?

Ananda No, I haven't ___ time yet, but I have ___ two other answers.

Sophie That's great. I've ___ that Brunel built Temple Meads Station.

Jo I'm sure you're right, Sophie. You're always right. But I need something to eat. I haven't ___ all day.

Ananda Well, what about the photos, Jo? Have you ___ any photos of the pirate pub yet?

Jo No, I haven't. Not yet. What about you? Have you ___ any texts?

Ananda No I haven't.

Jo So nobody has ___ much work yet.

Ananda Well, there's a lot of work to do. I need some help. Jo, if you aren't going to play football this afternoon, maybe ... Hey! Where's Jo? He was here a minute ago. Where is he? Sophie, have you ___ Jo?

5907 *Sophie* Hmmm. He's just ___ to the pirate pub for a pirate sandwich lunch.

Now you

1 What have you just done? *I've just finished exercise 7.*

2 What haven't you done yet today? ___

3 Have you ever been in a pirate pub? ___

4 What have you never done? But you would like to do it. ___

8 STUDY SKILLS Marking up a text ▸ p. 77 • SF (p. 127)

Mark up the text about John Cabot. Which information in each paragraph do you think is the most important? Think about:

1 when Cabot was young.
2 when he was a man.
3 what made him famous.
4 how people can remember him today.

Who was John Cabot?

He was born in Genoa, Italy in 1450, and his name was really Giovanni Caboto.
When John was young, his father told him stories about countries far away, and about Marco Polo. John wanted to be an explorer too. It was his dream to explore the world in a ship.

When John was a man, he moved with his family to Bristol, where there were a lot of ships. He planned to find a new sea route[1] to the west[2]. Some rich men in Bristol found his plans very interesting and they gave him money for a ship. He built a small but fast ship with the name 'Matthew'[3].

Cabot left from Bristol with his ship and 18 men in 1497. He wanted to find new land in the west. Six weeks later he found Newfoundland in Canada. When he came back to England, King Henry VII gave him some money. A year later Cabot left Bristol again for Newfoundland, now with five ships and 300 men. But this time he did not come back. Nobody heard of him again.

400 years later in 1897, the people of Bristol built the Cabot Tower to remember John Cabot, their 'Bristol explorer'. The red tower is 30 metres. You can climb to the top, and on a sunny day you have a beautiful view of the city.
There is also a Cabot Tower in St John's, Newfoundland, where John Cabot first landed.

9 Extra It's my turn, isn't it? (Question tags) ▸ p. 78 • GF 13 (p. 146)

What do they say? Choose the correct question tag and complete the speech bubbles.

wasn't it?	weren't you?	isn't she?	aren't you?	aren't they?	~~isn't it?~~

1 Now it's my turn, *isn't it* ?

2 No, Lucy! It was your turn last time, __________ ?

3 Becky, you're yellow, __________ ? Tim, that's Becky's counter!

4 Hey! That wasn't fair, Tim. You were on a snake, __________ ?

5 Oh, no! Lucy is the winner again, __________ ? She always wins.

6 That isn't fair! The winners are always the worst players, __________ ?

6009

[1]route [ru:t] *Route* [2]west [west] *Westen* [3]Matthew ['mæθju:]

10 At the juice bar

▸ p. 78

Read p. 78 in your student's book again. Write a dialogue between a customer and a waiter at the juice bar. Use the words in the box or your own ideas.

cherry • delicious • healthy • ~~help~~ • kiwi • large • medium • smoothie • sort • strawberry

Waiter Hello. How can I help you?

Customer I'd like __________.

Waiter __________

Customer __________

Waiter __________

6110 *Customer* __________

11 LISTENING Teamwork[1]

▸ p. 78 🎧 14

a) *Listen carefully to Tim, Becky and Florian. Then tick (✓) the correct box.*

	Right	Wrong	Don't know
1 Tim and his friends are going to write a report for school.	☐	✓	☐
2 They have to interview the sports teams.	☐	☐	☐
3 Florian takes good photos.	☐	☐	☐
4 Tim has got a new camera now.	☐	☐	☐
5 Florian wants to argue.	☐	☐	☐
6 Lucy is going to interview the judo team.	☐	☐	☐
7 Becky is in the junior tennis team.	☐	☐	☐
8 Florian is in the junior basketball team.	☐	☐	☐
9 Tim is going to check all the match results.	☐	☐	☐
10 Becky and Lucy are going to do all the computer work.	☐	☐	☐

6111

b) *Becky isn't happy about Tim's teamwork for the Sports Centre newspaper. Say why not. Write two or three sentences.*

____

____

____

____

[1] article ['a:tɪkl] *(Zeitungs-)Artikel*

12 STUDY SKILLS Structuring a text ▸ p. 79 • SF (p. 129)

Florian has written a text about the Bristol Balloon Fiesta. Read the text carefully and mark three paragraphs (beginning, middle and end) in three different colours.

Every year in August there's the Bristol Balloon Fiesta, Europe's biggest show of hot-air balloons[1]. It's the most exciting thing to do in Bristol in August. Hundreds of beautiful balloons from different countries meet – and about 500,000 visitors come to watch. It's great if the weather is good. If it's too windy, the balloons can't fly. But there's more than just balloon flights. There's a full programme of things to do and lots of fun things for kids too. Cool pop groups make live music and there are games, shows, prizes to win, a food market even a Wild West show and stunt cars. I've been to the Fiesta three times with my parents and friends. It's really cool to watch the balloons and you can take great photos.

13 WORDS Word bridges ▸ p. 79

How many words can you make from the word bridges? Use the Dictionary in your student's book (pp. 173–191).

c – r: calendar, clear, ______

p – r: painter, ______

w – r: waiter, ______

[1] hot-air balloon [ˌhɒt ˈeə bəˈluːn] *Heißluftballon*

14 WRITING An e-mail ▸ p. 79 • SF (p. 129)

*Imagine you were at the Bristol Balloon Fiesta too. Write an e-mail to a friend about it. Use ideas from Florian's text in exercise **12**. Don't forget to use **first**, **then**, **after that**, **in the afternoon**, etc. Write at least six sentences.*

Dear ______________________

Last weekend I went to the Bristol Balloon Fiesta with some friends. It's a hot-air balloon show.

I'll tell you about it.

First we ______________________

____

____

____

____

____

15 MEDIATION At the juice bar ▸ p. 79 • SF (p. 131)

Florian is with his cousin Heike and his German uncle and aunt in a juice bar. They don't speak much English. What does Florian say?

Waiter Hello, how can I help you today? As always we've got lots of different sorts of smoothies, all delicious. Our special smoothie today is cherry and banana. And of course, we've got our fruit juices and our special fruit salad.

Uncle Was hat er gesagt? Ich habe nichts verstanden. Der Typ redet zu viel und viel zu schnell.

Florian (to uncle): Er hat tolle Smoothies heute und Säfte auch. ______________________

Aunt Was hat er? Sm … Sm … Was ist das? Frag ihn bitte.

Florian (to waiter): My aunt ______________________

Waiter Oh, well, you make it with fruit and milk or ice cream. Delicious – and very healthy.

Florian (to aunt): Es wird ______________________

Uncle Heute muss immer alles gesund sein. Nein, danke. Ich nehme eine große Cola, bitte.

Florian (to waiter): My uncle ______________________

Aunt Und ich nehme so einen 'Schmusi'. Erdbeere, wenn sie es haben. Banane geht auch.

Florian My aunt ______________________

Heike Gute Idee. Für mich auch.

Florian OK. Dann nehme ich dasselbe. Alles groß, oder?

(to waiter): ______________________

16 WORKING WITH THE TEXT To catch a thief ▸ pp. 86–88

a) *Read pp. 86–88 in your student's book again. Who says what? Match the sentences to the speakers.*

Dan

- David can't find his mobile. Someone is stealing things from Form 8PK.
- Well, it can only be one person.
- And I don't think Lesley's a thief.
- We have to catch the thief and we need proof.
- And I put some money in the purse too. Five pounds.
- And you think this somebody is me.
- Hello, Mr Smith. What can I do for you?
- You really have to look after your things better, you know.
- Oh dear. Not one of the SHoCK Team's great cases, eh?
- We've learned that you always need proof before you go round and say people have stolen things, right Jo?

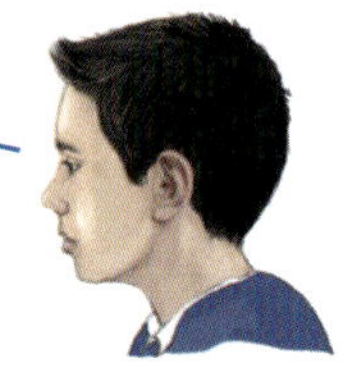

Jo

b) *Complete with beginnings or ends to make correct sentences.*

1 David's mobile was in the classsroom, but *then it disappeared / somebody took it.*

2 *Jo thought/said* ______ the thief was Lesley.

3 Jack was angry. He said, ______

4 'We're going to leave a purse with money in the classroom, and then ______

5 Sophie said, ______ – it bleeps when you whistle.'

6 'We put the key ring in the purse and ______

7 At the end of break Sophie whispered, ______

8 ______ the bleeps got louder.

9 Mr Smith opened his bag and ______

10 Mr Kingsley said, 'Mr Smith is right. You have to ______

c) *Was Jo fair to Lesley? Why or why not? Explain. Write a few sentences in your exercise book.*

I think Jo was/wasn't ...

1 What's the opposite?

1 open – ______ *4* clean – ______

2 rich – ______ *5* possible – ______

6501 *3* arrive – ______ *6* end – ______

2 What are they **going to do** today?

1 The twins ______.

2 Jo ______.

3 Sophie ______.

6502 *4* Ananda ______.

3 Complete the words.

Waiter Hi. How can I h______ you today?

C______ I'd like a smoothie, please.

W______ What s______ would you like?

Today we've got banana, strawberry, orange and kiwi too.

6503 They're all d______ and very h______.

4 Extra Circle the correct question tag.

Tim This is a cool juice bar, isn't it? / is it?

Lucy Yes, and the people are nice, isn't it? / aren't they?

Tim And it wasn't too expensive, wasn't it? / was it?

6504 *Lucy* And the smoothies were great, weren't they? / were they?

20 points

Now you

6505 *Do you like teamwork in projects? How many times have you done teamwork with classmates or friends?*

6506 *Write at least five sentences about teamwork in your exercise book.*

Unit 6 A trip to Bath

1 WORDS Lists and more ▸ pp. 92–93

a) *Write the words in the correct lists.*

Roman • room • jump • round • relax • stone • chat • cold • wall • have a bath • hot • have a sauna • statue • feel • warm • stairs • pool • dark

ADJECTIVES	NOUNS	VERBS
Roman	room	jump

6601

b) *Look at the pictures. What's happening? Use the mosaic pieces to make sentences to describe the pictures.*

1

2

is • pool • the • Roman • relaxing • hot • the • in • men • are • boy • Roman • into • jumping • cold • room

1 A Roman boy ____________________.

6602

2 Two ____________________.

2 WORDS Word building ▸ p. 94

a) *Which pairs go together? Find, colour and write the pairs.*

ticket	case	man	grand	centre	information	suit	ache
head	return	boots	sports	football	tourist	parents	police

One word: *suitcase,* ______

Two words: *return ticket,* ______

b) *What did Miss White and Mr Kingsley say before the trip to Bath? Complete with words from a).*

1 Miss White said, 'On the bus remember to buy a ______. It's cheaper.'

2 Mr Kingsley said, 'Stay together in Bath. But if you lose your group, ask a ______ for help.'

3 Miss White said, 'You can get some nice brochures of Bath from the ______.'

6702 4 Mr Kingsley said, 'No, Jo. You won't need your ______ in Bath. You can't play football!'

3 STUDY SKILLS Talking to people ▸ p. 94 • SF (p. 128)

Florian is talking to Mrs Baxter. Add phrases to make the dialogue more friendly. Choose from the box or use your own ideas.

Everything is fine. • You'll like it. • And how are you? • thanks (2x) • please
of course • That sounds interesting. • Have you ... before? • That's great.

Mrs B Tim will be back soon, Florian. How are you? Is everything OK?

Florian Yes, ______
______

Mrs B We're all fine too. I've just made some tea. Would you like some?

Florian Yes, ______.

Mrs B Sugar?

Florian No, ______.
We're going to Bath on a trip tomorrow.

Mrs B ______
______

Florian Yes, but I haven't seen the Baths yet. We're going to do that tomorrow. Have you seen them?

Mrs B Yes, ______. They're very interesting. But I think Tim liked the souvenir[2] shop a lot ...

Did you know?

Roman people said 'Salve!' when they met a friend. It means 'Hello!' in Latin[1].

[1] Latin ['lætɪn] *Latein* [2] souvenir [ˌsuːvə'nɪə] *Andenken, Souvenir*

4 WORDS Places in town ▸ p. 95

Which is which? Match the descriptions and colour the places. Use the same colours.

You can buy lots of different food and drinks here.	department store
There are lots of beds in this building.	police station
You can buy stamps here. You can also get money.	supermarket
You can go here for help if somebody has stolen your bike.	post office
You can spend lots of time and lots of money in this building. They've got everything.	chemist
You can buy things here if you have a cold, a headache or a sore throat. You can also buy things like make-up or soap.	hospital

6804

5 READING Where are the shops? ▸ p. 95

Lucy is telling Becky about some new shops. Read the dialogue carefully and write the names of the shops and the buildings on the street plan on p. 69.

Lucy Have you seen the new shops in Elm Street? There's a new department store, a chemist, a pizza restaurant, an internet café, …

Becky Hey, wait. Are there any clothes shops or shoe shops?

Lucy I think there's a clothes shop next to the post office, on the corner, and the shoe shop is next to the new chemist.

Becky And where's the pizza restaurant?

Lucy Hmmm, let me think. Oh, it's next to the cinema.

Becky And where's the internet café?

Lucy The internet café is between the post office and the new department store.

Becky And where's the new department store?

Lucy Oh, it's next to the internet café, on the corner, on the left. And you know where the police station is …?

Becky No, I don't know where the police station is.

Lucy Oh. Well, if you're standing in Elm Street in front of the new chemist, the police station is on the right. And the new pizza restaurant is on the left, on the corner.

Becky So the police station is behind the chemist and the shoe shop. Right?

Lucy Yes, that's right.

Becky Can you explain again, please, Lucy? That wasn't very clear.

Lucy OK. Well, if you're standing in front of the cinema, the restaurant is on the right. When you cross the street, you get to the department store. It's on the corner, on the left, next to the internet café, and the clothes shop is next to the post office, on the corner.

Becky Oh. Hmmm. Well, that's better. Now I understand. Why didn't you say that before?

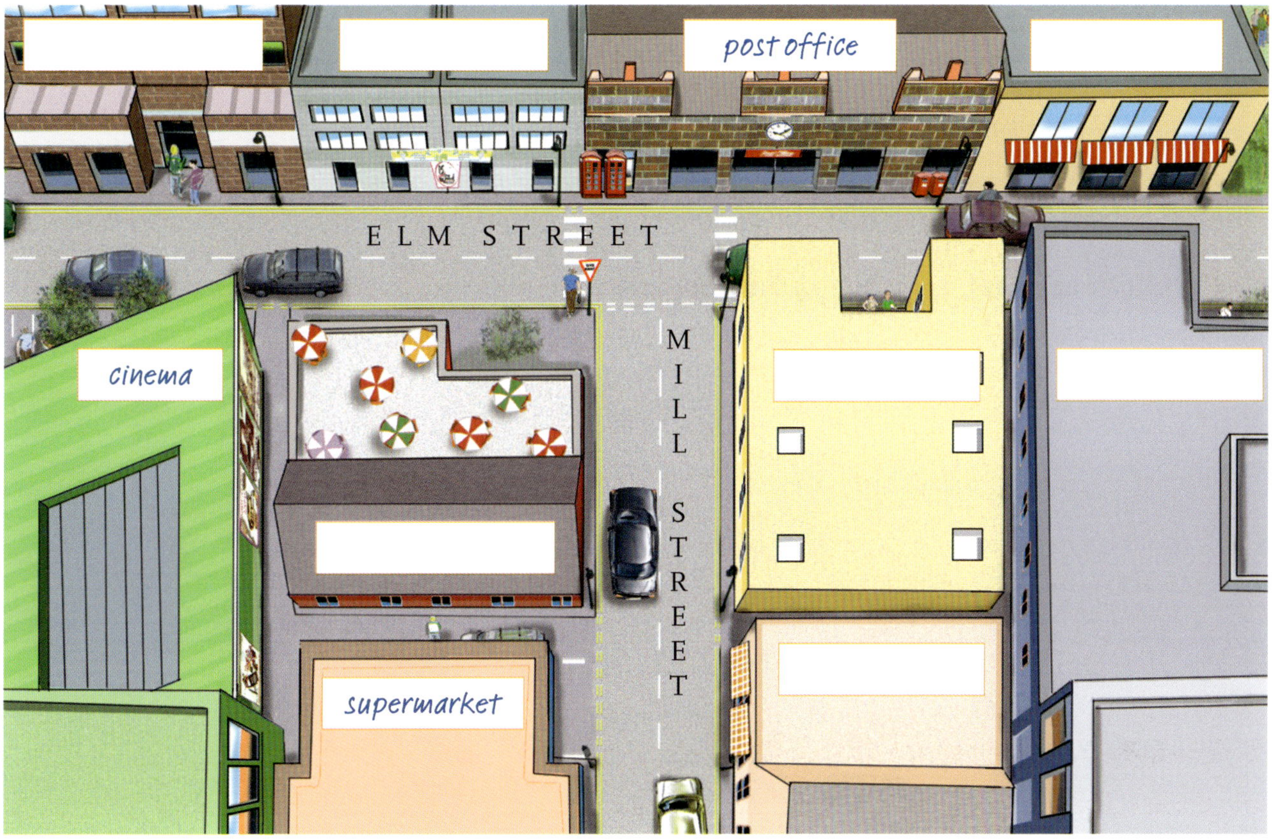

6 LISTENING Where's Elm Street? p. 95 15

Becky asks the way to Elm Street. Listen and draw the way on the map. Write the names of the streets and the buildings on the way there.

Now you

Choose a place you often walk to: your school, your friend's home, the nearest supermarket, … In your exercise book, explain how to get there from your home. You can use: **go past**, **turn right**, **turn left**, **go straight on**, **cross the road**, **on the right**/**left**, **on the corner of** …, …

To get to my friend's home, you go to the right and cross the road at … Street. Then you …

7 REVISION What are they doing today? (Present progressive)

▸ p. 96 • GF 14 (p. 146)

Today the sun is shining and the Muddles are in the garden. What is everybody doing? Write sentences with:

dance • feed • paint • play • shout • swim • wash

1 Max *is playing the guitar.*

2 Mr and Mrs Muddles ______________________.

3 Minnie and Millie ______________________.

4 Minnie ______________________.

5 Micky ______________________.

6 Molly ______________________.

7007 7 The neighbours ______________________.

8 What were they doing yesterday? (Past progressive) ▸ p. 96 • GF 15 (p. 147)

What were they doing at these times?

1 

8.00
make

At 8 o'clock Mrs Muddles *was making breakfast.* ____________

2 

8.30
walk/to school

At 8.30 Micky and Maggie ____________ .

3 

9.00
drive/to work

At 9 o'clock Mr Muddles ____________ .

4 

12.45
eat

At 12.45 Micky and Maggie ____________ .

5 

3.45
go

At 3.45 Max ____________ .

7108
7109

9 What was happening? (Past progressive) ▸ p. 96 • GF 15 (p. 147)

What was happening yesterday when Max looked through the pet shop window? Look carefully at the picture for two minutes. Then do the exercise on the next page.

Write what was happening when Max Muddles looked through the pet shop window. Use the words in the boxes.

try to get the fish	play with a snake	sing loudly	feed the dogs with dog biscuits
run round the shop	jump down from a cupboard	sit on a woman's head	fly round the shop

1 When Max looked through the window, a blue parrot was singing loudly.

2 ... a red parrot __________.

3 ... two boys __________.

4 ... a black cat __________.

5 ... four budgies __________.

6 ... a little girl __________.

7 ... lots of mice __________.

8 ... a black and white cat __________.

Now you

What were you and your family doing at 9 o'clock last night? Write a short paragraph.

At 9 o'clock last night I __________

Just for fun

As I was going to St Ives,
I met a man with seven wives.
The seven wives had seven cats.
The seven cats had seven rats[1].
Cats, rats, men, wives.
How many were going to St Ives?

[1] rat [ræt] *Ratte*

10 STUDY SKILLS Correcting mistakes

▸ p. 97 • SF (p. 130)

Here is an e-mail from Sophie's e-friend in Germany. In your exercise book, write it again without the spelling mistakes (blue). Look for three more spelling mistakes at the end of the text.

Deer Sophie

How are you? Is school OK? We went on a trip yesterday to the Deutsches Museum in Munich[1]. We went by bus and than on the underground. On the way their our teacher told us about the museum. There's so much to sea: planes, cars, old things, and a fantastic modell railway. I realy enjoyed it.

At lunch time we ate our sanwiches in the museum café. I bought too postcards from the book shop. I took some fotos of the most intresting things. There were lots of visiters. There was an english school class too. When we left, the wether was great. The sun was shineing, so the teacher bought us an ice creme. Today we had to right a report about the trip. Have you been on a trip too? Tell me about it.

7310 Love Angelika

11 WRITING My best/worst school trip

▸ p. 97

*Write an e-mail to your e-friend about your best or your worst school trip. For ideas look at Jo's report on p. 97 and exercise **11** on p. 102 of your student's book.*

[1] Munich ['mju:nɪk] *München*

13 QUIZ About Book 2 ▸ p. 97

a) *How quickly can you do this quiz? Circle the right answer. You need the numbers in brackets ( ) in part b).*

1 Who went to New York in the last summer holidays?

Dan and Jo. (5)	Ananda. (12)	Ananda and Dilip. (8)

2 Jody is …

Sophie's friend. (15)	the girl from St Ives. (1)	the new girl in 8PK. (7)

3 Whose mum lost her job?

Sophie's mum. (19)	Jack's mum. (16)	Ananda's mum. (22)

4 Who has a good idea for a project on recycling clothes?

Lesley. (16)	Ananda. (13)	Sophie. (5)

5 What does Ananda find in the yard?

Two baby frogs. (3)	Two baby hedgehogs. (25)	Two baby moles. (21)

6 Why is Scruffy in the Dogs Home? Because …

Lesley doesn't want him. (6)	Lesley's dad can't keep him. (8)	he ran away. (4)

7 Dan and Jo go to visit their grandparents in …

Bath. (1)	Wales. (15)	Cornwall. (18)

8 What does Emma make for the twins?

A fruit salad. (20)	A chocolate cake. (24)	A pie. (12)

9 The Thompsons don't go to the Brecon Beacons because …

Grandpa has no time. (19)	Jo wants to chat to his mum. (14)	Dan is ill. (9)

10 Who is Bryn?

A paramedic. (4)	A fireman. (5)	A policeman. (11)

11 Explore-at-Bristol is …

a pirate pub. (2)	a museum. (1)	a Georgian house. (17)

12 Who said: 'You really have to look after your things better, you know'?

Mr Hanson. (23)	Miss White. (16)	Mr Smith. (25)

13 In Bath Jack wants to visit the … with Miss White.

Theatre Royal (21)	Herschel Museum (19)	Museum of Costume (5)

○ ***b)*** *Now use the numbers in brackets ( ) after your answers to read the code. If your answers are correct, the letters make a message.*

1	2	3	4	5	6	7	8	9	10	11	12	13	14	15	16	17	18	19	20	21	22	23	24	25	26
A	B	C	D	E	F	G	H	I	J	K	L	M	N	O	P	Q	R	S	T	U	V	W	X	Y	Z

The message is: H ______________________________ !

1 Which parts go together?

Write four new words.

centre | post | store | station

police | department | office | leisure

1 ______________________ 3 ______________________

7501 2 ______________________ 4 ______________________

2 Correct the mistakes.

There's one spelling mistake in each sentence.

1 The sun was shineing when we left home. ______________________

2 On the bus everybody was chatting happyly. ______________________

3 The bus stoped near the museum. ______________________

7502 4 Suddenly Jo dissapeared. ______________________

3 Describe the pictures.

What were they doing yesterday at these times? Complete the sentences with the past progressive of **cycle**, **sit**, **take** *and* **wait**.

1 At 9.30 the students ______________ to Warmley.

2 At 10.25 they ______________ in the bus to Bath.

3 At 1.25 Miss White ______________ for her group.

7503 4 At 3.30 Jo ______________ photos.

4 Complete the words.

Ananda Excuse me, please. Can you tell me the w________ to the ice rink?

Woman Oh, well, I've got a m________ of Bath here, so I can show you where it is. Look. You go s________ on up this street, then you turn l________ into Old Roman Road.

7504 Go p________ the tourist information, then c________ the river into Park Road.

18 points

Now you

7505 *What do you think is good about school trips? What do you think is bad? Write two short paragraphs in your exercise book.*

7506 *Ideas:* **interesting**, **better than lessons**, **have fun with friends and teachers**, **boring**, **maybe weather bad**, ...

Jetzt kann ich ...	Sehr gut!	OK	Verbessern!
HÖREN: Ich kann ...			
... die Anweisungen, Fragen und Erklärungen meiner Lehrerin/ meines Lehrers verstehen.	☐	☐	☐
... mündliche Beiträge meiner Mitschüler/-innen verstehen.	☐	☐	☐
... die Listening-Aufgaben in meinem Buch/Workbook verstehen und bearbeiten.	☐	☐	☐
... die Vokabeln der Units 5 und 6 verstehen.	☐	☐	☐
... die Hörtexte der Units 5 und 6 auf meiner CD ohne Mühe verstehen.	☐	☐	☐
SPRECHEN: Ich kann ...			
... ein Brettspiel auf Englisch spielen, da ich dazu die notwendigen Vokabeln und Redewendungen beherrsche (z.B. *dice; It's your turn. Move back two spaces.*).	☐	☐	☐
... bei einer Diskussion in kurzen Sätzen meine Meinung zu einem Thema oder einer Geschichte sagen, auch wenn ich kleine Fehler mache.	☐	☐	☐
... korrekt und flüssig die Wörter der Units 5–6 aussprechen und anwenden.	☐	☐	☐
... nach dem Weg fragen und jemandem den Weg erklären.	☐	☐	☐
... mich freundlich auf Englisch unterhalten (z.B. mit *Yes, thank you. I'm fine, thanks. How are you? What about you? See you later.*).	☐	☐	☐
LESEN: Ich kann ...			
... die längeren Erzähltexte der Units 5 und 6 lesen und verstehen.	☐	☐	☐
... die längeren Erzähltexte der Units 5 und 6 ohne Mühe laut lesen.	☐	☐	☐
... längere Sachtexte lesen und verstehen.	☐	☐	☐
... Texte verstehen, indem ich versuche, unbekannte Wörter zu erschließen.	☐	☐	☐
SCHREIBEN: Ich kann ...			
... einen kurzen Bericht über eine Klassenfahrt schreiben.	☐	☐	☐
... einen kurzen Sachtext zu einem bekannten Thema schreiben.	☐	☐	☐
... meine Texte sinnvoll gliedern.	☐	☐	☐
... die Wörter der Units 5 und 6 richtig schreiben.	☐	☐	☐
LAND UND LEUTE: Ich habe ...			
... etwas über die Geschichte, über berühmte Menschen (z.B. Brunel, Blackbeard) und über die Sehenswürdigkeiten Bristols gelernt.	☐	☐	☐
... etwas über die Geschichte und Sehenswürdigkeiten Baths gelernt, z.B. über den Einfluss der Römer in und um Bath.	☐	☐	☐

Jetzt kann ich ...

	Sehr gut!	OK	Verbessern!
GRAMMATIKVERSTÄNDNIS: Ich kann ...			
... mit *am/are/is* + *going to* + Infinitiv über Absichten und Pläne für die Zukunft sprechen (z.B. *I'm going to start my project tomorrow.*).	☐	☐	☐
... die Verlaufsform der Vergangenheit *(past progressive)* richtig erkennen und bilden (z.B. *I was reading/they were writing*).	☐	☐	☐
... mit dem *past progressive* ausdrücken, dass etwas zu einem bestimmten Zeitpunkt in der Vergangenheit im Gange war (z.B. *Yesterday at 4 o'clock I was reading a book.*).	☐	☐	☐
VOKABELVERSTÄNDNIS: Ich kann ...			
... einige Wörter für Gebäude und Orte in der Stadt richtig verwenden (z.B. *post office, police station, hospital, market, ice rink*).	☐	☐	☐
... Wörter und Redewendungen, die ich für eine Wegbeschreibung brauche, richtig verwenden (z.B. *Can you tell me the way to ...?; turn right/left, go straight on*).	☐	☐	☐
SKILLS – LERNEN UND ARBEITEN: Ich ...			
... kann eine Multiple-Choice-Aufgabe bearbeiten.	☐	☐	☐
... kann einen Text markieren, um bestimmte Informationen zu kennzeichnen.	☐	☐	☐
... kann meine Texte in Einleitung, Mittelteil und Schluss gliedern.	☐	☐	☐
... weiß, wie ich am besten meine Texte auf Fehler und Verständlichkeit überprüfen kann.	☐	☐	☐

WAS ICH FÜR MEIN ENGLISCHLERNEN GETAN HABE: Ich habe ...	häufig	manchmal	nie
... den Unterrichtsstoff zu Hause noch einmal aufmerksam wiederholt.	☐	☐	☐
... mir viel Mühe mit meinen Hausaufgaben gegeben.	☐	☐	☐
... die vorgeschlagenen Aufgaben im Grammar File bearbeitet.	☐	☐	☐
... die vorgeschlagenen Aufgaben in meinem Skills File bearbeitet.	☐	☐	☐

WIE ICH MICH VERBESSERN KÖNNTE: Ich könnte ...

... mit den Listenings und den Pronunciation – Übungen in meinem Buch/Workbook meine Aussprache gezielt verbessern. ☐

... Sätze und Ausdrücke, die in bestimmten Situationen nützlich sind, auswendig lernen. ☐

... immer daran denken, meine Texte sinnvoll zu gliedern, d. h. in Einleitung, Mittelteil und Schluss. ☐

... immer daran denken, meine Absätze mit einem *topic sentence* zu beginnen. ☐

... so oft wie möglich versuchen, meine Englischkenntnisse aktiv einzusetzen, z.B. im Urlaub. ☐

- Hier kannst du deine Antworten im Checkpoint überprüfen. Falls du Probleme mit den jeweiligen Aufgaben hattest, folge den Lernhilfen in der rechten Spalte. Die Verweise beziehen sich auf dein Schülerbuch oder dein Workbook.
- Deine Punktzahl kannst du ermitteln, indem du dir für jede richtige Lösung einen Punkt gibst. Schreib deine Gesamtpunktzahl in das gelbe Kästchen unten links.

1 What's the weather like?

1 It's *rainy.*
2 *It's cloudy.*
3 *It's foggy.*
4 *It's windy.*

4 P.

- Schau dir im Skills File in deinem Buch den Punkt *Learning words - Step 1* (S. 121) noch einmal an.
- Lern die Wörter mithilfe des Vocabulary (S. 150–152).

2 That's wrong!

1 *Lesley didn't try to be nice.*
2 *She didn't want to come to Bristol.*
3 *Jack didn't fly to New York.*
4 *Jo didn't run to get help for Jody.*

4 P.

- Lies dir das Grammar File 2 (S. 134) zur Verneinung des *simple past* durch.
- Löse die Aufgabe 9 im Practice-Teil deines Buchs (S. 19). Wenn du diese Übung auf einem schwierigeren Niveau machen möchtest, schau dir S. 113 an.

3 Ask Ananda questions.

1 *Where did you go?*
2 *How long did you stay?*
3 *What was the weather like?*
4 *What did you do?*

4 P.

- Wie du Fragen im *simple past* bildest, kannst du im Grammar File 3 (S. 134) nachlesen.
- Wiederhole die Übung 13 im Practice-Teil (S. 21). Auf der S. 113 findest du diese Übung auch mit einem etwas schwierigeren Ansatz.

4 Describe the picture.

1 Ali is *on the right*.
2 Sue is *on the left*.
3 Pat is *between Sue and Ali*.
4 Ed is *behind Pat*.

4 P.

- Lern die Bedeutung und den Gebrauch dieser Wörter mithilfe der blauen Kästen im Vocabulary (S. 152).
- Mach die Aufgabe 2 im Practice-Teil (S. 16) noch einmal.

Now you (Musterlösung)

On the first day of school after the holidays we got a new form teacher. First he/she gave us our new timetable, but he/she didn't give us any homework. Then I saw my old friends and we talked about the holidays. We got some new books for English, German and Maths, but we didn't do much work.

- Falls du Schwierigkeiten hattest, einen zusammenhängenden Text zu schreiben, schau dir im Skills File den Abschnitt zu *Linking words* (S. 129) an.
- Wiederhole die Übung 6 im Practice-Teil (S. 18).
- Schreib deinen Text zur Aufgabe 9 im Workbook (S. 8) noch einmal in dein Heft.
- Lern die Formen des *simple past* (Grammar Files 1–2, S. 133–134).

Ich habe ______ Punkte von 16.

16–14	Sehr gut. Weiter so!
13–11	Schon recht gut.
Unter 11	Genauer lernen!

Falls du Probleme hattest:

1 Clothes: write the names.

1 skirt
2 dress
3 shirt
4 trousers
5 (baseball) cap
6 jacket

6 P.

- Schau dir im Skills File den Abschnitt zu *Learning words - Step 1* (S. 121) noch einmal an.
- Lern die Wörter mithilfe des Vocabulary (S. 155–156).
- Löse die Aufgabe 2a–b im Practice-Teil (S. 32).

2 Find group words for these things.

1 subjects
2 free-time activities
3 head
4 clothes

4 P.

- Schau dir im Skills File den Punkt *Learning words - Step 2* (S. 121) noch einmal an.
- Wiederhole die Übung 1 im Practice-Teil (S. 32).

3 Complete with *mine*, *yours*, …

1 *Tim* Is this old jacket yours, Becky?
2 *Becky* No, it isn't mine. Ask Mum. Maybe it's hers. Or ask Dad.
3 *Tim* Ask Dad? It isn't his. It's pink with little white rabbits!

4 P.

- Lies dir im Vocabulary (S. 156) den blauen Kasten zu Possessivpronomen durch.
- Löse die Aufgabe 3 im Practice-Teil (S. 32). Diese Übung gibt es auch etwas schwieriger (S. 113).

4 Compare with *than*.

1 Art – Music: easy
I think… is easier than…
2 detective stories – animal stories: exciting
I think… are more exciting than…
3 Sophie – Emily: nice
I think… is nicer than…
4 the Simpsons – Mr Bean: funny
I think… is/are funnier than…
5 a summer holiday – a holiday in the snow: good
I think… is better than…
6 a boring Sunday – a long school day: bad
I think… is worse than…

6 P.

- Im Grammar File 4 (S. 135–136) findest du Informationen zur Steigerung der Adjektive.
- Wiederhole die Übungen 9a (S. 35) und 12 (S. 36) im Practice-Teil.

Now you (Musterlösung)

I spend my pocket money on comics or magazines. I don't buy clothes or stuff for school. Sometimes I buy sweets and drinks or ice cream after school. I spend most money on magazines and cinema tickets. I don't get much pocket money, so I don't save much.

- Schau dir im Skills File den Abschnitt zu *Mind maps* (S. 122) an. Dort erfährst du, wie du deine Ideen sammeln und ordnen kannst.
- Die Schülerbuchseiten 26–27 können dir inhaltliche Informationen liefern.

Ich habe ____ Punkte von 20.

20–17	Sehr gut. Weiter so!
16–13	Schon recht gut.
Unter 13	Genauer lernen!

1 What is it?

1 *a squirrel*
2 *a monkey*
3 *a hippo*
4 *a bear*
5 *a deer*
6 *a lion*

6 P.

Falls du Probleme hattest:

- Schau dir im Skills File die Punkte *Learning words - Step 1* und *Step 2* (S. 121) noch einmal an.
- Lern die Wörter mithilfe des Vocabulary (S. 159–160).
- Wiederhole die Übung 1a im Practice-Teil (S. 48).

2 What will the weather be like?

1 In England it *'ll* be sunny and it *won't* rain.
2 In Scotland it *'ll* rain, but it *won't* be cold.

4 P.

- Die Formen und den Gebrauch des *will-future* findest du im Grammar File 5 (S. 137).
- Löse die Aufgaben 2a (S. 48) und 3a (S. 49) im Practice-Teil. Wenn du die Übung 2a auf einem schwierigeren Niveau machen möchtest, schau dir S. 114 an.

3 What will happen if …?

1 If I *find* (find) a hedgehog baby, I *'ll have to* (have to) give it water.
2 It *'ll get ill* (get ill) if I *give* (give) it milk.
3 If I *give* (give) it cat food it *'ll survive* (survive).

6 P.

- Die Bedingungssätze (Typ 1) werden im Grammar File 6 (S. 138) erklärt.
- Üben kannst du sie, indem du die Aufgabe 5 im Practice-Teil (S. 50) wiederholst.

4 Describe the pictures.

1 Dan is running *quickly*.
2 Sophie is riding her bike *carefully*.
3 Ananda is working *quietly*.
4 Mr Kingsley is shouting *angrily*.

4 P.

- Wie du die Adverbien der Art und Weise bildest und verwendest, erfährst du im Grammar File 7 (S. 139–140).
- Löse die Aufgabe 11 im Practice-Teil (S. 52) noch einmal. Auf S. 115 findest du diese Übung auf einem etwas schwierigeren Niveau.

Now you (Musterlösung)

When I'm 25, I think I'll still live in Germany. I'll have an interesting job, but maybe I won't live in the same town. I think I'll have a little car, but I won't have a big house or a plane. Maybe I'll speak very good English, but I won't work in England.

- Schau dir die Formen und den Gebrauch des *will-future* im Grammar File 5 (S. 137) noch einmal an.
- Der Punkt *Mind maps* im Skills File (S. 122) gibt dir Informationen, wie du deine Ideen sammeln und ordnen kannst.

Ich habe ______ Punkte von 20.

20–17	Sehr gut. Weiter so!
16–13	Schon recht gut.
Unter 13	Genauer lernen!

1 What's in the picture?

1 river
2 sheep
3 factory
4 castle
5 railway
6 field

6 P.

Falls du Probleme hattest:

- Schau dir im Skills File die Punkte *Learning words - Step 1* und *Step 2* (S. 121) noch einmal an.
- Lern die Wörter mithilfe des Vocabulary (S. 162).
- Wiederhole die Übung 1b im Practice-Teil (S. 64).

2 Write correct sentences.

1 I'll be at the station at five-thirty.
2 We were in the DVD shop till six.

2 P.

- Über die Wortstellung informiert dich das Grammar File 8 (S. 141).
- Löse die Aufgaben 2 und 3 im Practice-Teil (S. 64), um sicherer Sätze bilden zu können.

3 What have they done?

1 Ananda has found a hedgehog.
2 Jo has dropped some glasses.
3 The Thompsons have packed a picnic.
4 Emma has made a pie

4 P.

- Schau dir die Grammar Files 9–10 (S. 142–143) an, um den Gebrauch und die Formen des *present perfect* besser zu beherrschen.
- Um sicherer im Gebrauch zu werden, mach die Übungen 7–9 im Practice-Teil (S. 66–67). Die Aufgaben 7a und 8 gibt es auf den S. 115–116 auch auf einem etwas schwierigeren Niveau.

4 Complete the words.

Mum Tim, what's the m atter?
Are you feeling i ll?
Tim Yes, my throat h urts and I have a t emperature. And my head. I have a terrible h eadache. And my legs hurt when I m ove. I can't go to school today.
Tim Really? But the French test is today …

6 P.

- Lies dir in deinem Schülerbuch die S. 62 noch einmal durch. Dort findest du Redewendungen, die man benutzt, wenn man krank ist.
- Lern diese Wörter mithilfe des Vocabulary (S. 163–164).

Now you (Musterlösung)

Germany is a big country. About 83 million people live here. Lots of people visit Germany too. Berlin is the biggest city. About 3.5 million people live there. There are many interesting places to visit and lots of things to do. You can visit museums, churches, theatres and old buildings. Germany is a beautiful country too. It has got nice cities and lakes, sea and beaches too. The biggest mountain is the Zugspitze. It's 2,962 metres. You can go up the mountain on a railway, or you can walk!

- Falls du Schwierigkeiten hattest, einen zusammenhängenden Text zu schreiben, schau dir im Skills File den Punkt zu *Mind maps* (S. 122) und *Topic sentence* (S. 129) an.
- Die Übung 5 im Practice-Teil (S. 65) kann dir dabei helfen, deinen Text besser zu strukturieren.

Ich habe ____ Punkte von 18.

18–16	Sehr gut. Weiter so!
15–13	Schon recht gut.
Unter 13	Genauer lernen!

1 What's the opposite?

1 open – closed
2 rich – poor
3 arrive – leave
4 clean – dirty
5 possible – impossible
6 end – beginning

6 P.

Falls du Probleme hattest:

- Schau dir im Skills File die Abschnitte zu *Learning words - Step 1* und *Step 2* (S. 121) noch einmal an.
- Du findest diese Gegensatzpaare im Vocabulary mit diesen zwei schwarzen Pfeilen ◂ ▸ (S. 162, 166–168).

2 What are they going to do today?

1 The twins are going to play football.
2 Jo is going to take photos.
3 Sophie is going to read about Blackbeard/a book.
4 Ananda is going to write texts.

4 P.

- Wie du das *going to-future* richtig formst und verwendest, erfährst du im Grammar File 12 (S. 145).
- Löse die Aufgaben 3 und 4a im Practice-Teil (S. 81), um besser im Gebrauch des *going to-future* zu werden. Wenn du die Übung 3 etwas schwieriger haben möchtest, schau auf S. 116.

3 Complete the words.

Waiter Hi. How can I help you today?

Customer I'd like a smoothie, please.

Waiter What sort would you like? Today we've got banana, strawberry, orange and kiwi too. They're all delicious and very healthy.

6 P.

- Lies dir die S. 78 in deinem Buch noch einmal durch. Dort erfährst du, wie man sich ein Getränk bestellen kann.
- Lern die Wörter mithilfe des Vocabulary (S. 166–167).

4 Extra Circle the correct question tag.

Tim This is a cool juice bar, (isn't it?) / is it?

Lucy Yes, and the people are nice, isn't it? / (aren't they?)

Tim And it wasn't too expensive, wasn't it? / (was it?)

Lucy And the smoothies were great, (weren't they?) / were they?

4 P.

- Im Grammar File 13 (S. 146) erfährst du, wie man *question tags* richtig verwendet.
- Übe den Gebrauch der *question tags* mithilfe der Aufgabe 10 im Practice-Teil (S. 84).

Now you (Musterlösung)

I like teamwork. It's nice to talk about ideas and do work with classmates. I have done teamwork for German. It's interesting to do teamwork for projects. Everybody in the team can find out different information from the internet. You can do a presentation in teamwork too.

- Schau dir im Skills File den Abschnitt zu *Mind maps* (S. 122) an, um deine Gedanken besser ordnen zu können.
- Denk an ein Projekt/eine Arbeit in der Schule, das/die du im Teamwork gemacht hast.

Ich habe ______ Punkte von 20.

20–17	Sehr gut. Weiter so!
16–13	Schon recht gut.
Unter 13	Genauer lernen!

Falls du Probleme hattest:

1 Which parts go together?

1 leisure centre
2 post office
3 department store
4 police station

4 P.

- Schau dir im Skills File die Punkte *Learning words - Step 1* und *Step 2* (S. 121) noch einmal an.
- Lern diese Wörter mithilfe des Vocabulary (S. 157, 170–172).
- Löse die Aufgabe 2 im Practice-Teil (S. 98).

2 Correct the mistakes.

1 shining
2 happily
3 stopped
4 disappeared

4 P.

- Lies im Skills File die Seite zu *Correcting mistakes* (S. 130).
- Wiederhole die Übung 11a im Practice-Teil (S. 102).

3 Describe the pictures.

1 At 9.30 the students were cycling to Warmley.
2 At 10.25 they were sitting in the bus to Bath.
3 At 1.25 Miss White was waiting for her group.
4 At 3.30 Jo was taking photos.

4 P.

- Im Grammar File 15 (S. 147) erfährst du, wie du das *past progressive* formst und wann du es verwendest.
- Üben kannst du das *past progressive* mithilfe der Aufgaben 7 und 8 im Practice-Teil (S. 100–101). Wenn du diese beiden Aufgaben etwas schwieriger haben möchtest, schau auf die S. 118–119.

4 Complete the words.

Ananda Excuse me, please. Can you tell me the w ay to the ice rink?

Woman Oh, well, I've got a m ap of Bath here, so I can show you where it is. Look. You go s traight on up this street, then you turn l eft into Old Roman Road. Go p ast the tourist information, then c ross the river into Park Road.

6 P.

- Schau dir die S. 95 in deinem Buch noch einmal an. Dort findest du die Redewendungen, die du brauchst, um nach dem Weg zu fragen oder einen Weg zu beschreiben.
- Such dir in deiner Umgebung eine Straße/ein Gebäude aus und beschreibe von deiner Wohnung/deinem Haus aus den Weg dorthin.

Now you (Musterlösung)

School trips are interesting. You can go to a museum or visit an old town and see something new. You can have fun with friends and teachers. It's better than lessons.
School trips can be boring too. Maybe it's cold and rainy, but you have to go. You have to stay together with the class and with the teachers.

- Mit einer Mindmap (Skills File, S. 122) solltest du zuerst deine Gedanken zu Klassenfahrten/-ausflügen sammeln und ordnen.
- Auf der S. 129 im Skills File findest du Hilfestellungen, wie du deinen Text geschickt mit *linking words* verbindest, deinen Text in Absätze einteilst und deine Absätze einleitest.

Ich habe ______ Punkte von 18.

18–16	Sehr gut. Weiter so!
15–11	Schon recht gut.
Unter 11	Genauer lernen!

Unit 1

GF 1 REVISION The simple past: positive statements ▸ *GF (pp. 133–134)*

We **were** in Spain **last summer**. It **was** great. We **went** swimming a lot and **played** volleyball on the beach.
Wir waren letzten Sommer in Spanien/sind letzten Sommer in Spanien gewesen ...

Mit dem *simple past* kannst du über Vergangenes berichten, z.B. wenn du eine Geschichte erzählst.
Das *simple past* steht häufig mit Zeitangaben wie *last summer, yesterday, three weeks ago, in 2004*.

a) (to) be and regular verbs

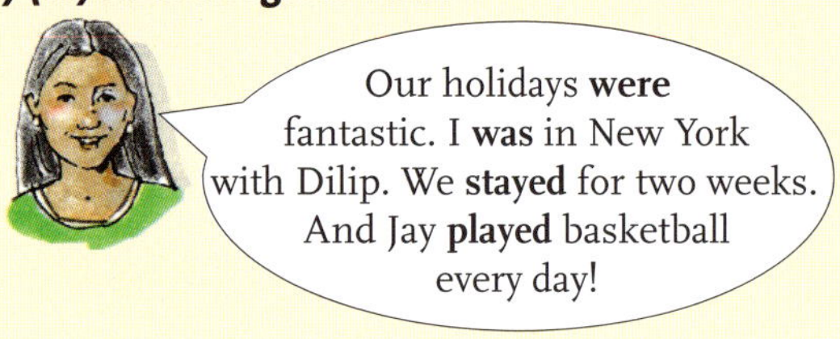

Beim *simple past* von ***be*** gibt es nur zwei Formen:
I, he/she/it *was* ***you, we, they*** *were*

Bei **regelmäßigen Verben** bildest du das *simple past* durch Anhängen von ***ed*** an den Infinitiv:
stay → *stayed*, *play* → *played*

Es gibt für **alle** Personen nur eine Form.

b) Irregular verbs

The Carter-Browns **went** to Majorca.
(Infinitiv: **go**)
Dan and Jo **met** a nice girl in Cornwall.
(Infinitiv: **meet**)

Wie im Deutschen gibt es auch im Englischen eine Reihe von unregelmäßigen Verben, deren *simple past*-Formen du einzeln lernen musst.

▸ *Unregelmäßige Verben (pp. 210–211)*

GF 2 The simple past: negative statements ▸ *GF (p. 134)*

Sophie: Lesley **didn't want** to come to Bristol.
Ananda: She **didn't say** much.
But we **didn't ask** her much.

Eine Aussage im *simple past* verneinst du immer mit ***didn't*** **+ *Infinitiv*** (Langform: *did not*).

Merke:	**Simple present**	I don't **get up** early.	Lesley doesn't **get up** early.
	Simple past	I didn't **get up** early.	Lesley didn't **get up** early.

GF 3 The simple past: questions and short answers ▸ *GF (p. 134)*

Did Jo **help** Jody? – Yes, he did./No, he didn't.
Did the girls **talk** to Lesley? – Yes, they did./ No, they didn't.
Why did Jody **need** help?
How did Dan **help** her?

Fragen im *simple past* bildest du mit ***did***:
Did Jo help?
! (Nicht: Did Jo ~~helped~~?)

Das Fragewort steht wie immer am Anfang.

Merke:	**Simple present**	Do you **get up** early?	Does Lesley **get up** early?
	Simple past	Did you **get up** early?	Did Lesley **get up** early?

Unit 2

GF 4 The comparison of adjectives ▸ *GF (pp. 135–136)*

a) Comparison with *-er/-est*

How old are the Carter-Brown children?
– Well, Sophie is young. She's twelve. Toby is younger. He's nine. Baby Hannah is the youngest, and Emily is the oldest.

Steigerungsformen verwendest du, um Personen oder Dinge miteinander zu vergleichen, z.B.:

young [jʌŋ]	jung
younger ['jʌŋgə]	jünger
(the) youngest ['jʌŋgɪst]	der/die/das jüngste ...; am jüngsten
old	alt
older	älter
(the) oldest	der/die/das älteste ...; am ältesten

Die Steigerung mit ***-er/-est*** verwendest du für
– einsilbige Adjektive (*young, full, nice, big*, ...) und
– zweisilbige Adjektive mit der Endung ***-y*** (*pretty, funny, easy*, ...).

b) Comparison with *more/most*

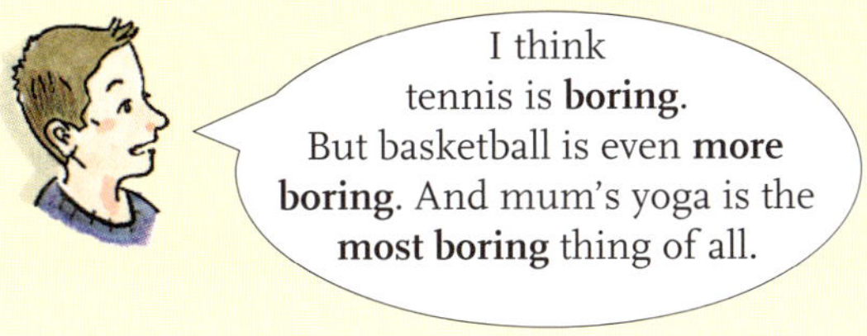

Andere Adjektive werden mit ***more*** und ***most*** gesteigert:

boring	langweilig
more boring	langweiliger
(the) most boring	der/die/das langweiligste ...; am langweiligsten

Weitere Beispiele:

expensive	–	*more expensive*	–	*most expensive*
diffucult	–	*more difficult*	–	*most difficult*

c) Irregular comparison

Ananda has got a good idea, but Sophie's idea is better. Lesley has got the best idea.

Jo hasn't got much money this week. Dan has got more, but Dilip has got the most.

Einige Adjektive werden unregelmäßig gesteigert:

good	–	*better*	–	*best*
bad	–	*worse* [wɜːs]	–	*worst* [wɜːst]
much/many	–	*more*	–	*most*

Die Steigerung der Adjektive

Mit *-er/-est*:	Mit *more/most*:	Unregelmäßig:
Einsilbige Adjektive:	Andere zwei- und mehrsilbige Adjektive:	
old – older – oldest	*boring – more boring – most boring*	*good – better – best*
Adjektive auf *-y*:	*terrible – more terrible – most terrible*	*bad – worse – worst*
happy – happier – happiest	*exciting – more exciting – most exciting*	*much/many – more – most*

d) bigger than – as big as

Is your cat as **fast** as my rabbit?
Ist deine Katze so schnell wie mein Kaninchen?

◂ Wenn Personen oder Dinge **unterschiedlich** groß/schnell/alt/... sind, vergleichst du sie mit der 1. Steigerungsform + ***than*** („als"):

Your rabbit is	*bigger*	*than*	*my cat.*	(... größer als ...)
Your cat is	*faster*	*than*	*Hip.*	(... schneller als ...)

▲ 1. Steigerungsform

! (Nicht: ... *bigger/faster ~~as~~* ...)

◂ Wenn Personen oder Dinge **gleich** groß/schnell/alt/... sind, vergleichst du sie mit ***as*** *big/fast/old/...* ***as***.
(Verneint: *not as big/fast/old/... as*)

Unit 3

GF 5 The *will*-future

▸ *GF (p. 137)*

Ananda: **What** will **they** need?
Will **they** want **milk?**
Sophie: **No, they** won't.

Ananda: I want to help the hedgehogs.
I will send an e-mail to the Animal Hotline.

Um auszudrücken, was in der Zukunft geschehen wird, benutzt du ***will*** + **Infinitiv**. Es gibt für **alle** Personen nur eine Form.
Die Kurzform von *will* ist *'ll*: *I'll, you'll* usw.

Das *will-future* steht häufig mit Zeitangaben wie *tomorrow, next month, soon, in a few weeks*.

Die **verneinte Form** von *will* heißt ***won't***. (Langform: *will not*).

Fragen kannst du **mit Fragewort** (*What will they ...?*) oder **ohne Fragewort** (*Will they ...?*) stellen.
Die Kurzantworten lauten: *Yes, I will / No, I won't* usw.

! Nicht verwechseln:
– *I want to* heißt „ich will".
– *I will* heißt „ich werde".

GF 6 Conditional sentences (type 1) ▸ *GF (p. 138)*

If you **give** a hedgehog water, it**'ll be** happy.

Wenn du einem Igel Wasser gibst, wird er zufrieden sein.

If you **don't keep** it warm, it **won't survive**.

Wenn du ihn nicht warm hältst, wird er nicht überleben.

Bedingungssätze (Typ 1) sind „Was ist, wenn ...“-Sätze: Sie beschreiben, was unter bestimmten Bedingungen geschieht oder nicht geschieht.

Die Bedingung steht im *if*-Satz, die Folge davon steht im Hauptsatz:

***if*-Satz** (Bedingung) ▼	**Hauptsatz** (Folge für die Zukunft) ▼
*If you **give** a hedgehog water,*	*it**'ll be** happy.*
*If you **don't keep** it warm,*	*it **won't survive**.*
Im *if*-Satz steht das *simple present*.	Im Hauptsatz steht meist das *will-future*.

GF 7 Adverbs of manner ▸ *GF (pp. 139–140)*

a) Use

Hedgehogs are **slow** and **quiet**.

◂ Ein **Adjektiv** beschreibt ein **Nomen** näher.

Hedgehogs walk slowly and quietly.

◂ Ein **Adverb der Art und Weise** beschreibt ein **Verb** näher.

b) Regular forms

Adjektiv			Adverb
slow	→	slowly	
quiet	→	quietly	
careful	→	carefully	

Die meisten Adverbien der Art und Weise entstehen durch Anhängen von *-ly* an das Adjektiv.

c) Irregular forms

She did a **good** job with the babies. (Adjektiv)
She did the job well. (Adverb)

Jo: The rabbits are very **fast**. (Adjektiv)
Dan: Of course! All rabbits can run fast. (Adverb)

Ananda: It's **hard** work at the clinic. (Adjektiv)
Steve: The volunteers at the clinic work very hard. (Adverb)

Einige Adverbien haben eine unregelmäßige Form, die du auswendig lernen musst.

– Das Adverb zu *good* heißt *well*.

– Bei *fast* und *hard* sind Adjektiv und Adverb gleich.

d) Word order

'You killed the hedgehogs,' she shouted angrily.

Steve fed **the babies** carefully.

Steve fütterte vorsichtig die Babys.

Das Adverb der Art und Weise steht direkt **nach dem Verb**.

! In Sätzen mit Objekt steht es **nach dem Objekt**.

Unit 4

GF 8 Word order ▸ *GF (p. 141)*

a) REVISION S – V – O

Jack **writes stories**.

Die Wortstellung im Aussagesatz lautet S – V – O (Subjekt – Verb – Objekt): *Jack writes stories.*

What do you do **when you** come **home**?
Was machst du, **wenn du nach Hause** kommst?

Auch im Nebensatz ist die Wortstellung **S – V – O**.
Denk dabei an die **Straßen-Verkehrs-Ordnung**, an die du dich immer halten musst!

b) Place before time

We can go **to the mountains in the morning.**

Wir können morgen Vormittag in die Berge fahren.

Wenn Ortsangaben (*to the mountains*) und Zeitangaben (*in the morning*) zusammen am Satzende stehen, dann gilt: **Ort vor Zeit**.

1	2
Ort	**Zeit**
... to the mountains	*in the morning.*

GF 9 The present perfect: use ▸ *GF (p. 142)*

Hurry up, boys! I**'ve cooked** bacon and eggs and Grandpa **has packed** a picnic.

Mit dem *present perfect* drückst du aus, dass jemand etwas getan hat oder dass etwas geschehen ist. Dabei ist **nicht wichtig**, **wann** es geschehen ist. Deshalb wird auch kein genauer Zeitpunkt genannt.

Wenn du aber den genauen Zeitpunkt angeben willst (*yesterday, last week, two years ago, in 2004*), musst du das *simple past* verwenden.

GF 10 The present perfect: form ▸ *GF (pp. 142–143)*

a) The past participle

1 Grandpa **has** packed a picnic.

They **have** planned a day in the mountains.
Dan and Jo **haven't** tidied their room.

2 The twins **haven't** seen Caerphilly Castle.
Dan doesn't feel well, so he **hasn't** eaten his breakfast.

Das *present perfect* wird mit *have/has* und der 3. Form des Verbs gebildet. Die 3. Form des Verbs heißt **Partizip Perfekt** (*past participle*).

1 Bei regelmäßigen Verben hängst du ***ed*** an den Infinitiv an:
pack + ed → *packed*.

◂ Beachte die Besonderheiten der Schreibung und der Aussprache (siehe GF 1, S. 133).

2 Unregelmäßige Verben haben eigene Formen, die du einzeln lernen musst. Unregelmäßige Verben werden immer so angegeben: *(to) see, saw,* ***seen*** *(to) eat, ate,* ***eaten***.
Die 3. Form ist das *past participle*.

▸ *Unregelmäßige Verben (pp. 210–211)*

b) Positive and negative statements

1 The neighbours have made a pie for the Thompsons.

2 Grandpa hasn't cleaned the car yet.

1 Bejahte Aussagesätze im *present perfect*:
have/has + **Partizip Perfekt**.

2 Verneinte Aussagesätze im *present perfect*:
haven't/hasn't + **Partizip Perfekt**.

Positive statements		**Negative statements**		**Long forms**
I've packed		I haven't seen		I/You/We/They have (not) packed
You've packed		You haven't seen		He/She has (not) packed
He's packed		He hasn't seen		
She's packed	a picnic.	She hasn't seen	Dan.	I/You/We/They have (not) seen
We've packed		We haven't seen		He/She has (not) seen
You've packed		You haven't seen		
They've packed		They haven't seen		

c) Questions and short answers

Have the twins been to the Brecon Beacons?
– Yes, they have./No, they haven't.

Bei Fragen im *present perfect* werden Subjekt und *have/has* vertauscht.

Has Jo installed the software?
– Yes, he has. / No, he hasn't.

Kurzantworten werden mit *have/has* gebildet.

Why has Grandma printed out the instructions?

Fragewörter stehen wie immer am Satzanfang.

GF 11 The present perfect with adverbs of indefinite time ▸ *GF (p. 144)*

Grandpa: I've **already** packed the car.
Ich habe schon das Auto beladen.

Grandma: Oh, good. Have the twins had breakfast **yet**?
Haben ... schon gefrühstückt?

Grandpa: I've **just** seen Jo in the kitchen. But Dan has**n't** come down **yet**.
Ich habe gerade Jo ... gesehen. Aber Dan ist noch nicht nach unten gekommen..

Das *present perfect* drückt aus, dass etwas irgendwann geschehen ist. Daher findest du oft **Adverbien der unbestimmten Zeit** in *present perfect*-Sätzen:

already	schon, bereits
just	gerade (eben), soeben
not ... yet	noch nicht
ever?	jemals? / schon mal?
yet?	schon?

Die Adverbien der unbestimmten Zeit stehen **direkt vor** dem *past participle*.

! Ausnahme: *yet* steht am Satzende.

Unit 5

GF 12 The *going to*-future ▸ *GF (p. 145)*

Jo: I'**m going to take** the photos tomorrow and Ananda **is going to do** the computer work.
Ich werde morgen die Fotos machen und Ananda hat vor, die Computerarbeiten zu erledigen.

Wenn du über **Absichten un[…]ne** für die Zukunft sprechen willst, verwendest du das Futur mit *[…]ing to*.
Es wird mit ***am/are/is* + *going* […] + Infinitiv** gebildet.
Die Kurzformen heißen *I'm/you're/he's going to* usw.

Positive statements		Negative statements		Questions and short answers
I'm going to		I'm not going to		Are you going to watch TV?
You're going to		You aren't going to		– Yes, I am. / No, I'm not.
He's/She's going to	read.	He/She isn't going to	play.	
We're going to		We aren't going to		Is Jo going to watch TV?
You're going to		You aren't going to		– Yes, he is. / No, he isn't.
They're going to		They aren't going to		

GF 13 Extra Question tags with *be* ▸ *GF (p. 146)*

bejaht ▼ … verneint ▼
There's a table in the corner, **isn't there**?

◂ Wenn der Aussagesatz bejaht ist, ist das Frageanhängsel verneint.

verneint ▼ … bejaht ▼
It isn't too expensive here, **is it**?
Look at the prices before we sit down.

◂ Wenn der Aussagesatz verneint ist, ist das Frageanhängsel bejaht.

Unit 6

GF 14 REVISION The present progressive ▸ *GF (p. 146)*

What **are** you **doing**, Jo?

Was machst du gerade, Jo?

Das *present progressive* wird mit *am/are/is* + *-ing*-Form des Verbs gebildet.
Die *-ing*-Form ist der Infinitiv + *-ing*: ***do*** → ***doing***, ***wait*** → ***waiting***.
Beachte: ***have*** → ***having***, ***plan*** → ***planning***

GF 15 The past progressive ▸ *GF (p. 147)*

Yesterday at one o'clock Form 8PK and their teachers were having lunch.
Gestern um ein Uhr aßen die Klasse 8PK und ihre Lehrer gerade zu Mittag.

Mit dem *past progressive* drückt man aus, dass etwas zu einem bestimmten Zeitpunkt in der Vergangenheit gerade im Gange war.
Es wird mit *was/were* + *-ing*-Form gebildet.

Jack was telling jokes, but Jo wasn't listening.

◂ Die verneinten Formen heißen *I wasn't listening/ you weren't listening/he wasn't listening* usw.

What was Jo doing? Was he talking to Ananda?
– No, he wasn't. He was planning a trick.

◂ Fragen kannst du **mit Fragewort** (*What ...?*) oder **ohne Fragewort** (*Was he ...?*) stellen.
Die Kurzantworten sind *Yes, I was / No, I wasn't* usw.